Hot Chocolate at Hanselmann's

D0149978

Hot Chocolate
at
Hanselmann's

ROSETTA LOY

Translated and with an introduction by Gregory Conti

UNIVERSITY OF NEBRASKA PRESS
LINCOLN & LONDON

Publication of this book was
assisted by a grant from the
National Endowment for
the Arts

NATIONAL
ENDOWMENT
FOR THE ARTS

Cioccolata da Hanselmann
© 1995 R.C.S. Libri & Grandi
Opere S.p.A., Milano; © 1997
RCS Libri S.p.A., Milano

Translation and introduction
© 2003 by the University of
Nebraska Press

Manufactured in the United
States of America

Cataloging-in-Publication
Data Available
Library of Congress Control
Number: 2002031958
ISBN 0-8032-2945-3 (cl.: alk. pa.);
ISBN 0-8032-8006-8 (pa.: alk. pa.)

N

Pity would be no more,
If we did not make somebody Poor:
And Mercy no more could be,
If all were as happy as we: . . .

William Blake, THE HUMAN ABSTRACT

Contents

Translator's Introduction

The Italian word *storia* means both "story" and "history." It is also commonly used to refer to what English speakers might call an "affair," or a "love story," or in more recent times perhaps, a "relationship." *Hot Chocolate at Hanselmann's* comprises all these meanings of *storia* and explores their various interconnections.

Much of the history involved in the narrative—World War II and the Holocaust—will be familiar to American readers. But some of it, particularly the persecution and rescue of Jews in Italy and Italian-occupied southern France, may not be, just as it was not well known to Italian readers when the book was first published in 1995. Unlike Germany, whose Nazi government directed and carried out the extermination of the Jews, and the United States, which welcomed a large number of Jewish survivors, Italy did not begin to examine seriously its own role in the Holocaust until the 1990s. With the possible exception of Giorgio Bassani's *The Garden of the Finzi-Continis*, which focused on post-1943 Nazi-occupied Italy, Rosetta Loy's novel *Cioccolata da Hanselmann* was the first important fictional treatment of Italian persecution of Italian Jews.

Arturo Cohen, the son of a Jewish-Italian father and a gentile, foreign mother, is a young professor of biology at the University of Rome. When the story begins in 1938, Arturo is about to lose his teaching position as a consequence of the racial laws soon to be issued by the Fascist regime. The racial laws were promulgated starting on 14 July 1943 with the publication of the "scientists' manifesto," which declared Jews biologically extraneous to the national community. Subsequently, pursuant to decrees issued at an ever faster pace, foreign Jews were expelled from the country and Italian Jews were banned from public schools, the army, and the professions. Mixed marriages were prohibited, increasingly greater shares of property were confiscated, and Jews were prohibited from, among other things, owning radios and using public transportation. Then in September 1943, following the Nazi occupation of the peninsula, Italian Jews began to be deported to concentration camps.

The racial laws make it impossible for Arturo to continue living in Italy, and he seeks refuge in nearby southern France. When the Germans set up the puppet regime in Vichy, Arturo returns briefly to Rome, but he then goes back to France, first to Marseilles and later to Nice. At the time, Nice is occupied by the Italian army, and Arturo remains in that city until September 1943, when Italy breaks its alliance with Germany and Italian troops are forced to withdraw from France. Arturo's stay in France and his work as a forger of false documents for Jewish refugees offers readers a glimpse of what the American historian Susan Zuccotti has called the "paradox of wartime Italy": while Italian Jews were persecuted in Italy, in Italian-occupied France (as in Croatia and Greece) the Italian army and the diplomatic corps did everything possible to protect Jews from deportation and death.

Arturo is the only Jew and the most important male figure in a story otherwise dominated by women and girls who are Catholic. Loy's original title for the book was "The Guest" (discarded when she discovered it had already been used by another Italian writer). The dominance of the women juxtaposes and subordinates the masculine world of "history"—politics and law, war and diplomacy— to the intimate, feminine sphere of family, a world in which Arturo is at times a welcome guest, at times a suspect intruder, but always an outsider. Arturo is first introduced as a friend of the family of his university colleague Enrico, his wife, Isabella, and their two daughters, Lorenza and Marta. After his escape from France, Arturo finds refuge in Switzerland with Isabella's half sister, Margot, their mother, Signora Arnitz, her granddaughter Marisetta, and another male "guest," Eddy, the son of Signora Arnitz's lover.

The family has been a major theme throughout Loy's work ever since her first novel, *La bicicletta*, was published in 1974, when Loy was 43 and raising her four children. She is also the youngest of four children of a well-to-do Catholic family born of a Roman mother and a Piedmontese father who, like Arturo's colleague Enrico, opposed fascism but nevertheless failed to protest against Mussolini's persecution of the Jews. "I have an ambivalent attitude toward the family," Loy stated in a 1995 interview. "I see it as both refuge and prison. I don't ever forget, however, that it is the only place that gives us a sense of belonging, the place where we clash with others and form our own identity. There is no way to do without the family. We still haven't found anything that, for better or worse, can take its place."

Arturo's love stories with Isabella and Margot bring public history into the realm of family history where the confrontation between the ways that he and the sisters respond to his persecution provides a focal point for Loy's reflections on the differing ethical stances of Catholicism and Judaism. "One of the things that induced me to write *Hot Chocolate at Hanselmann's*," Loy says, "is precisely this contrast between Catholics and Jews. Catholics very easily feel pity but it's not as easy for them to feel a sense of justice, as is the case for Jews. This leads, in my view, to helping the victims but not to demanding justice before they become victims."

The bridge between the two branches of the family—Isabella's in Rome and Margot's in Switzerland—and hence between the public sphere of Arturo's persecution and escape and the private sphere of his love stories with Isabella and Margot, is Lorenza, Isabella's daughter and Margot's niece. Lorenza is both a witness who spies on the adult world with the curious eyes of childhood and a historian/storyteller who later, as a young woman, composes the book's contrapuntal narrative of public and family history. Since she is not an eyewitness to all of the events that she recounts, Lorenza must rely on a series of accounts composed or told to her by others—Arturo, Margot, her grandmother—and the result is a complex narrative structure that jumps forward and backward in time, constantly forcing Lorenza, the other characters, and the reader to revise their interpretations of people and events in light of new information, or rather in light of the rediscovery of pieces of the past that have been cast aside in the relentless forward march of time.

One Italian reviewer has compared this narrative development to the spiral movement of a traditional waltz, where the women continually change partners as the music plays on. The choice of a musical metaphor is apt as music figures prominently throughout the story and rhythm is an all-important element in the telling of the tale. But the interplay of past and present, between the weight of memory and the impact of present perception, is also reflected in the recurring geometric images—a jigsaw puzzle, a kaleidoscope, Russian matryoshka dolls—which also remind us, as the narrator comments, that mathematics and music "are bound to one another by rhythm and formulas, by geometric compositions and abstract beauty."

The complexity of the narrative structure is counterbalanced by the unobtrusive elegance of Rosetta Loy's prose. Her Italian reviewers consistently refer to the "luminous quality" of her writing, calling it "sober and measured" and finely attentive to "allusive detail and the precision of the particular." The narrator never imposes herself on the story but limits herself to following and accompanying the unfolding of events. It may seem paradoxical, given Loy's profound emotional involvement with the moral and political issues of her generation, but American readers may find her prose style more reminiscent of writers of an earlier generation, such as Edith Wharton or Willa Cather, rather than of a writer from the postmodern late twentieth century.

In response to an interviewer who asked how much of the novel was autobiographical, Rosetta Loy replied that none of it was, except the apartment where she grew up on Via Flaminia in Rome and the "gaze of the little girl who investigates everything that is happening around her. I've always been a kind of active spectator." This translation tries to apply the same approach, to take a position, as it were, looking over the shoulder of the narrator, to try to reconstruct in English the measured elegance of the original Italian while retaining as much as possible of the Italian syntax and structure and paying special attention to the rhythm of the phrasing. In keeping with this strategy, a choice was made to maintain Italian forms of address for family members, to leave foreign words and phrases (in French, German, or Latin) in their original form, and, on a few occasions, to render Italian idiomatic phrases in a literal translation rather than use a similar idiomatic expression in English. The intention is to invite the reader to become an "active spectator" too, not only of the events described in the narrative, but also of the act of narration. Unlike the reader of the original work, the reader of the translation has access to another level of spectatorship, the level of watching the story unfold as it is being told to its original audience, an audience that shares the language and culture of the storyteller. If from time to time the reader of the translation feels like an observer of a storytelling performance, the translation will have achieved its objective.

PART 1

Arturo was a friend of Papà's. Mamma liked him a lot too, but she always ended up liking the same things her husband did. The two girls thought he was comical, and those evenings when he came over for dinner they would spy on him from behind the piano that sat across the corner at one end of the dining room. When Mamma left their room after shutting off the light, they would slip out of bed and stand in the doorway that opened into that dead corner, taking turns gluing their eyes to the narrow opening between the piano and the wall. The three of them were over there, in the opposite corner by the radio, and the walnut wainscoting seemed to gather in their voices, not letting so much as a whisper get away. Papà always sat in a sort of reclining chair with raised velvet flowers, one hand holding up an ankle while the other one, abandoned on the arm of the chair, sent up a pale blue spiral of cigarette smoke. Arturo, meanwhile, could never sit still. He stood up, sat back down, put his hands in his pockets, and every so often, to accentuate the effect of what he was saying, he would make the strangest faces. And then Mamma, sitting on a stiff, low-backed armchair, would laugh and shake her blond head in disbelief.

Arturo was a colleague of Papà's. They both taught, one biology and the other mathematics; similar subjects, Mamma said, but also very different. Arturo had a lot more to do with animals, the oceans, and the sky. Every time he came to dinner he brought a package tied up with a string, and the strangest things might be inside. Rushing to unwrap it, the girls would sometimes find a chocolate bar; but other times there was only a clothespin or a cookie—just one. Otherwise what kind of surprise would it be? he would say, and his dark black eyes, set deep under his eyebrows, would stare into theirs—whether joking or stern they could never tell—his hair bristling straight up on his head.

He was younger than Papà and didn't wear neckties, and his sweaters had the most extravagant colors; red, pea green, and yellow. Who knows where he goes to buy them, Mamma used to say, and Papà was a little jealous because when Arturo was around she was always more cheerful. Sometimes the three of them went out together, and the girls would watch from the window as they got on the tram or walked arm in arm, Mamma in the middle, on their way to Piazza del Popolo. "It's too bad you married Enrico," he said one time, "You would have been an extraordinary *allumeuse*." Mamma turned red, and a look of defiance came over her face; but when the girls asked her what *allumeuse* meant, she answered right away: "Someone who warms people's hearts." "A lot more than their hearts," Arturo protested; he laughed and his big, irregular teeth gave him the carefree look of a boy. Then the red blush on Mamma's cheeks shot right up to her temples.

All of his students at the university are in love with him, Papà used to say, that's why he hasn't got ahead in his career. They make him waste so much time. Often on Sundays they would sit together on the long bench in front of the piano, and while Arturo played, Papà would turn the pages for him. Other times just the two of them would go to a concert or to the opera, like that Sunday when the young soprano, Simoniato, sang in Thomas's *Mignon*. Mamma didn't go with them; she couldn't stand sitting still for all that time without being able even to shift her legs or blow her nose. The few times she did go, she was immediately seized with an urge to cough. And at the opera she couldn't keep her eyes open, falling into a dead sleep.

Music is the only thing we don't have in common, Papà would say to her, but you'll see, sooner or later I'll make you like that too.

4

Sometimes on Sunday, after Papà had gone out with Arturo, Mamma took the girls to the park on the Pincio to see the puppet show. Arlecchino and Pulcinella going after each other like cats and dogs, banging their wooden heads all over the stage, or the Proud Princess with her yellow wool tresses beseeching the King-her-Father not to make her marry the beggar. The girls laughed and clapped their hands, and she sat on a bench waiting for them, her gaze lost among the expanse of rooftops beyond the balustrade. Different from the other mothers, foreign and melancholy. And when the curtain came down and Pulcinella popped out swinging a tin can hanging on a string, the girls would run over to her to ask for some change, impatient because they thought she wasn't opening her purse fast enough.

Sometimes Arturo would sit down at the piano by himself and play the Swiss national anthem for her. His strong-fingered hands would strike the keys heavily, as his lean, olive face took on a solemn expression. Then all of a sudden he would start thumping up and down the keyboard as if he were playing a polka, and his wide boyish mouth would curl up into a mischievous grin, with a look that seemed to plunge right to the bottom of her delighted, cheerful laugh. Almost as if happiness itself consisted in snatching that little trumpet blast of a sound out of her throat. But it might also happen that he would play an old French song for her that went *Isabelle, si le Roi savait ça, a la robe de dentelle, tu n'aurais jamais plus droit, Isabelle, si le Roi savait ça* . . . and then the mockery turned into a veil over his face, becoming thinner and thinner as his eyes gazed at her lips, her neck, ran down along the soft body under her dress, and then came back up to meet her eyes again, with an inquiring look.

It was always difficult with him to know if he was serious or not. He had a long, angular face that changed expression very easily and made you forget its oversized mouth. When he was in a good mood he would treat the girls to an imitation of Laurel and Hardy and the

5

words seemed to come right out of his belly. But he tired of it quickly; girls that's enough now, he would say, I'm not the court jester. And in an instant he could make them feel terrible, as if some unfathomable distance had somehow inserted itself between him and them, and the girls had all of a sudden become incredibly small, almost invisible in his eyes.

He always ended up staying for dinner on Sunday evening, even though he knew there wouldn't be any surprises. Sunday was Aldina's night off and when she closed the door behind her at four o'clock, dressed in her black overcoat adorned with a collar made from some poor unidentified beast, she left the dinner already prepared, the bloodless chicken neck sticking out of the pan amid round eyes of fat floating on the surface of the broth.

All Mamma had to do was buy the olive oil rolls. But every Sunday it seemed as though it were the first time Arturo had ever seen the capellini in the soup tureen, or picked up the porous, slithery-skinned chicken thigh from the serving plate. And he ate everything with the same indifferent voracity, the emerald green figs and ruby red cherries of the Cremona mustard sauce disappearing along with the topaz pears into his huge mouth. If he was cheery the girls laughed from the soup to the fruit and Mamma forgot about trying to teach them good table manners. They played the clown as much as he did. But there was an elusiveness in the back of his eyes, an absence, a dark black point of no return that could grab hold of any spontaneous impulse and stop it cold. Then he would sit silently in front of his bowl, carefully rolling up the capellini against his spoon as if he were performing some ritual act that required the most intense concentration. Mamma and Papà would leave him alone with his thoughts, their phrases passing listlessly back and forth, flimsy and opaque.

Other times, but they were rare, a wrong word or an apparently harmless comment brought everything to a halt. Arturo's mood would change completely from one moment to the next. But there

6

was no way to prevent it from happening. It happened and that was it. And the girls would be left with their mouths full of food, unable to swallow. Then Arturo's deep-set, dark black eyes would look away, and in the sudden silence it seemed they could hear the sound of his teeth.

It was the winter that Lorenza and Marta came down with the measles; from one week to the next Arturo stopped coming. It was as if he had vaporized among the trams and delivery trucks, the tricycles that clogged the traffic most of the day on Via Flaminia. The last time the girls had seen him, Arturo was sitting by the radio with Papà. They were arguing, and all of sudden Arturo raised his voice. Papà tried to maintain a measured tone, calm. In the opening between the piano and the wall the girls could see him holding his ankle in his usual pose; but his body was all hard and stiff, his vest crumpled up into folds where his belly should have been. A belly Papà doesn't have, has never had, lean as he is. Arturo stood up and then sat back down and took a cigarette out of the leather case, but his hands were shaking and he couldn't light it, and then suddenly his eyes, shiny as marble, looked over toward the piano. Maybe he had seen, above the piano, that the door was ajar. Maybe he'd even seen the girls themselves, their noses stuck in the crack of the door. Mamma brought in some more coffee and set the tray on the table, busying herself immediately with emptying the ashtrays full of cigarette butts. "Take it easy for a minute," Papà said to her, "Sit down." His voice was harsh but she seemed unable to stop herself and disappeared, the dark wool of her dress showing the dandruff on her shoulders. The girls couldn't see her anymore. Arturo called her, the name Isabella breaking off in his throat. But all of a sudden she was coming toward the piano, her eyes transfixing Marta and Lorenza in their little hiding place like two tongues of fire. They ran into bed, pulling the covers up over their heads. Mamma came into the room, her body a black figure against the

7

light from the hallway, her blond curls a fiery halo: "All right, are you going to sleep or not?" The girls squeezed their eyes shut; she went straight to the door, still ajar behind the piano, and turned the key several times. Then she walked off, holding the key tight in her fist.

For a while after that night the girls still leaned out over the railing on the balcony hoping to see him arrive with his swaying gait and his jacket unbuttoned over a pea green sweater. Then Papà told them it was useless, *Arturo is gone*. Mamma put the felt back on the piano keyboard and once in a while some other colleagues of Papà's came over and Mamma would stay and sit with them for a few minutes, but then she always found some excuse to get up and start doing something else. They, Enrico's colleagues, would follow her with their eyes, her wool dress snug around her round, fleshy hips, those long legs, full in the calf and thin and sinewy at the ankles.

It was more or less around that time that Isabella began to develop a passion for music. Perhaps out of love for Enrico. Or to keep faith with a promise. Or for yet some other reason. Enrico would be surprised to see her sitting beside him as she listened, motionless, to a Beethoven symphony, her profile supported by her thin neck, and her slightly long chin raised toward the orchestra. She follows the frenetic movement of the violins looking lost, her round knees emerging from the silk of her dress, her big white hands, with their easily split nails, gripping the program. Where is she, where has she gone in her mind, entrusting the notes with her innermost thoughts, the emotion of her inexpressible desires?

But Enrico has won, he has succeeded in getting her to love music. He doesn't ask himself at what price. And before going to hear Gieseking or Backhaus he explains the various phases of the concerto to her and the importance of the movements composing it. He sings a few notes of one of the themes, his fingers tracing out the imaginary tempo in the air as she listens to him, her myopic eyes

8

squinting between her eyelashes with the concentration of someone who doesn't want to miss a thing of what's being explained to her. Details that up to that time had left her utterly indifferent, obtuse: the same indifference and obtuseness that she's always shown for mathematics. Mathematics and music, Isabella knows well, are bound to one another by rhythm and formulas, by geometric compositions and abstract beauty. They come together and split apart again in the mind, without passing through the heart. The heart is base, it pulls one down amid impulses and dreams.

Later, at home, however, while Enrico wants to keep talking about the sonatas and the symphonies, still inspired and impassioned by the memory, she seems suddenly to have lost all interest. The girls, she says; their homework. And she keeps the programs from the concerts in perfect order, as if in waiting, on top of the piano.

Enrico doesn't go to the opera anymore. Two seats in the orchestra are too expensive, he has declared, and he refuses to take Isabella to those places where one is packed in among other people's body odors, those hidden away seats way up high, where one ends up seeing hardly anything. Isabella, he always says, is like the princess in the fable, reduced to taking the geese out to pasture while she waits to be recognized as the wife of the king. Only he's been left without a crown, somebody else has taken his place on the throne. There's no king for Isabella who used to play with her golden ball in His Majesty's garden. Mamma laughs as her hands crumple up the program with the list of performances that will be held during the season at the Royal Opera House. And when the program has finally been completely scrunched, she remembers that she could very well have used it as a sheet of notepaper. Isabella, the beauty, who has lost her golden ball and is now forced to do the daily accounting of income and expenses, the lire that come and go in her change purse.

And when Enrico wants to hear the *Elisir d'amore* or the *Ballo in maschera* he patiently puts one record after another on the radio-gramophone and listens to them, absorbed on the velvet-flowered reclining chair, while she moves busily around the house. Sometimes, when the voices from the dining room rise up thundering and full of torment, lost in love, she is intent on turning the toenail scissors around some photograph in an illustrated magazine. The twentieth, the thirtieth, she herself doesn't even know anymore; and the feverish hands of her elder daughter rip it immediately out of her fingers to glue it into a photo album lying open among the rumpled sheets. Flitting about here and there on those pages all sticky with glue are tennis players in the limelight, animals at the zoo, and a bevy of big-breasted ladies. Other, thinner women, like the Duchess of Windsor, walk lightly down the coconut gangway of an ocean liner while the Dionne quintuplets sit like so many dolls, all lined up in a row. The girl's hand pushes hard to flatten them out on the page and in the meantime the thermometer in her groin pops out between her skinny thighs and gets lost among the covers. It breaks. And Mamma loses her patience, sick and tired of cutting up magazines, of chasing after poisonous little spheres of mercury on the bed. That voice, those entreaties, those gloomy orchestral crashes exploding through the house.

Doctor Vannutelli comes and taps two fingers on the little girl's bony back; puts his cold, hairy ear against her scalding hot skin. What she needs is some good mountain air, he always says, at least two months in the mountains. He's an old Alpine trooper who fought on Piz Boè and up in the Tofanes, and he believes in the special qualities of the higher climes and the virgin winds that blow down from the glaciers. But Mamma doesn't. She comes from the country of watches and cheese, as the concierge calls it, where the purity of the uncontaminated mountain peaks, along with the ruck-sack, had been the nightmare of her childhood. "She's a lymphatic child," she protests, "Maybe the sea would do her good." "What are you talking about, lymphatic? Look here." Doctor Vannutelli's fat finger pulls down Lorenza's lower eyelid, turns her feverish lip inside out. "This is called lack of iron, of red blood cells. Rare meat, and plenty of good air. Anyway, next week she can go outside."

But the next week Lorenza has an earache and, all curled up in her parents' big double bed, she looks into the crystal mirror on the wardrobe where a ray of sunlight breaks up into the colors of the rainbow. The fresh, clear light of spring comes in through the barely opened window (oh this Swiss mania for fresh air! Papà protests every time he walks in front of an open window), and when a puff of wind lifts the curtain, a blaze of diamonds glistens in the mirror. Mamma comes and goes, her shoes squeaking against the parquet floor. She changes the plaster on her ear. She has a letter in her hand. "Who's that from?" her little girl asks. "From Arturo." "So how long will he be away?" "He doesn't know." "And the university, all those students who are in love with him?" (She's very sensitive when it comes to love and at the cinema she cries over the images of unhappy lovers.) "He doesn't teach at the university anymore," Mamma answers abruptly, "and the girls will get over it." She walks around with that letter in her hand as if it were a handkerchief and then she leaves it on the dresser and turns her attention to something else. Lorenza looks at that white sheet of paper bathed in the azure breath of the sunlight, and thinks about the times when the three of them would go out together and she and Marta would wave to them from the balcony, envious of Mamma in her lavender scarf between Papà and Arturo. The letter is now a butterfly, fluttering in the breeze, Mamma comes over to her to replace the plaster with a warmer one and the little girl pulls her head back. "It burns," she snaps, and Mamma blows on it, squeezing her lips into a heart shape. One time Lorenza overheard Arturo and her speaking French, and Mamma kept shaking her head like she was scolding him for something. Then all of a sudden she turned red and her eyelids started quivering in that way the little girl knows so well.

2

Was she beautiful? What a beautiful mother you have! some sales girl would exclaim while she wrapped up something Mamma had just purchased, smiling at her as if she were sure to be an accomplice in the admiration. But Lorenza thought she was too fat; and she didn't like those pointy lips that she painted bright red in front of the mirror, her myopic eyes squinting to keep the color from spreading beyond its proper place. A while ago, yes, she would have said that she was beautiful and perfect in every part of her body; but not anymore. And as the car climbed through the Majola pass, swaying around the curves and making her sick to her stomach, her critical glance came to rest on that slightly beaked nose, not pretty at all.

It was raining and the tires skidded as the motor gasped and roared. It was already dark and the water was streaming in torrents down the narrow gorge. Every now and then Lorenza would let out a long sigh of discomfort, but Mamma, sitting next to her on the seat, pretended not to notice, her gloved hand grasping the armrest, squeezing tighter at every curve. Her mouth locked in the sort of grimace that Lorenza detests, like the slit of a piggy bank cut into her powdered white face. Then she started to slide her hands along the folds of her mother's dress and with every jolt of the car, when their bodies involuntarily slid up against each other, her fingers would sink down into the cold silk. A hand that was asking for a little comfort; but her mother, intent on the road outside, seemed not even to see it, her little blond curls shining bright, barely jiggling in the midst of all of that careening. And when Lorenza couldn't help herself from letting out a sigh that was louder than the others, she kept on, cruelly looking at the road, her bird-like profile set against the darkness.

Chesa Silvascina appeared suddenly as the car came to a halt in the gravel driveway: two stories in wood set on a foundation of big, light-colored stones; and in the vast clearing whose outlines faded into the distant trees, the last light of the day showed it with its windows all lit up, looking like squares of gold on the rain-darkened wood. Mamma paid the driver under the noisy drumming of the water on her umbrella; and then that same umbrella dripped on the carpet in the entryway until a little puddle formed around its tip. Finally, it was warm!

Mamma looked all around as if she wanted to check to see how much was left intact of a place she both loved and hated, but then voices that seemed to emanate from every corner of the house came together sharply in the stairwell, the lights came on, and footsteps came scrambling down the stairs. Mamma stood erect in her overcoat spotted with rain, slowly removing her hat, while Lorenza was almost knocked off her feet by the forceful handshakes of two girls and a boy, their names bouncing around from one to another.

Signora Arnitz was the last to arrive, coming out from the room the little girl would learn to call "the living," and Mamma turned all red, her hands holding onto the hat she didn't know where to put. The kiss they exchanged was quick and light and then Signora Arnitz took the little girl's hands and patted them as if she were testing their consistency: *Aber unmöglich, wie dünn sie ist!* One of the few phrases in German that Lorenza was to hear her speak over the next few months. Small, fat, with crispy hair, half blond half gray, buttery skin still firm around her cheeks. So this was the grandmother that her father called "la Semiramide." She smelled like the woods, like strawberries.

"Don't be silly," Mamma said once they were in their room, "It's 'Arpège,' by Lanvin." She lay down on a yellow chaise longue and looked, disconsolate, out the window at the still, dark sky, "She's

14

never used any other perfume." She was exhausted. But Lorenza was cheerful again and walked around the room skimming her fingers along the canvas of the foliage-patterned wallpaper; at the slight pressure from her hand, a hidden door, camouflaged by the cloth, opened with a little click onto the bathroom, almost as large as the bedroom. Lorenza turned the handle above the bathtub and water gushed out from the gold faucet shaped like the jaws of a lion and tumbled around the long, deep basin. "And did you see the two girls?" she yelled out to be heard above the sound of the water, "Do you think they'll play with me sometimes even though they're older than me?" "Don't talk from one room to another, come here." Mamma squinted as if trying to bring her into focus. "Come here," she said again, her legs stretched out on the chaise and her silk stockings glowing like honey in the half-light. Lorenza sat down beside her and Mamma hugged her. For the first time that day she felt the cuddly warmth of her body. Too late, too late; she sat there in her arms, inert and awkward.

Vivia. Marisetta. Proud as tigers, sitting at the table, indifferent to the common mortals, they spoke with the boy in a lingo that was almost incomprehensible; fast, made up of allusions and words that seemed invented, not the least bit concerned about interrupting Nonna. And whenever they felt like it they would stick their fingers in the food or laugh out loud, showing off what they were chewing while the maid stood there waiting with a plate in her hands.

The object of their attention and hilarity was Eddy. His glasses formed two ridiculous looking circles on his wide, pudgy face and he just sat there playing the dunce. But every now and again his slightly crossed eyes flashed into focus behind the lenses and his fingers flicked one of the little dough balls he had lined up beside his plate. The ball would land in the serving dish or in one of the girls' water glasses and he would sit there laughing silently, his soft lips opened to show his straight, compact teeth, little and white. An angelically beautiful mouth.

Instead of taking offense or reprimanding them, Signora Arnitz was amused, lightly tapping a knife or fork against her glass whenever the din became excessive. She had changed for dinner and her wide, black velvet lapels highlighted the pink-white of her face where her small eyes, rimmed with eyeliner but almost no eyelashes, azure blue like the "veil of the Madonna," stood out like pins. Her hair, however, looked as though she had forgotten about it. It went off in all directions, thick and dull, held together badly by a few hairpins. And instead of calling her Nonna or Signora Arnitz the girls addressed her with the abstruse *Mamigna*.

Confined in front of their plates, under the light of an overhead lamp shaped like two gigantic deer antlers, Lorenza and Mamma sank into nothingness; and Mamma responded to Nonna's pallid attempts to start up a conversation with occasional monosyllables as she kept eating, slowly and cautiously as if the food might have been poisoned.

Margot wasn't there that night and there was a lot of talk at the dinner table about her going on a trek to the Roseg glacier that required several days. "If she'd known you were going to stay for only one night," Signora Arnitz said, "I'm sure she would have put it off. She's been looking forward to your visit for weeks." "I'm really sorry about it too," Mamma answered. But she seemed to be saying it just for appearances, as if the missed meeting didn't bother her at all.

At the sound of Margot's name Eddy stopped paying attention to Vivia and Marisetta. "The trek to Roseg is fantastic," he said, "If this damned cough hadn't come back again I would have gone too," and his cross-eyed glance reached the little girl and her mother at the end of the table without their being able to understand which of the two he was looking at.

Lorenza would not meet Margot, the only child born of Nonna's second marriage, until two days later. By that time Mamma had already left with her felt hat over her blond curls and a last, chased-after kiss as the car rolled over the crunching gravel, Lorenza's hand grabbing on to the window, not wanting to let go of Mamma's big white hand.

Sitting on the little wall looking down at the swimming pool, Lorenza saw her come up out of the water and shake her wet head like a dog might do, standing on the edge of the pool paved with big gray stones. She rubbed the towel back and forth forcefully across her back as the little girl, all bundled up in a sweater, watched her, biting into the last piece of bread and butter from breakfast. "You're Aunt Margot, right?" she asked, letting some crumbs fall down on the railing. "Yes, but just call me Margot." "Margot, Margherita . . ." Lorenza began to singsong; she seemed to have the luster of a fresh daisy, the glow of that morning light with the sun still hidden behind the mountain. As if she had read her mind, Margot let the towel slide down to the ground, her blue wool bathing suit showing off her body with its slender waist and firm thighs. There was nothing fat about that body, just fullness, strong like a young man's, "Margherita is also the name of a precious stone," she said, "*Ne proicias margaritas ante porcos . . .*" and her mouth contracted into a laugh that was jittery with cold, her lips violet

Eddy was crazy about her. When he arrived that morning in his robe and Margot had already gone, a disconsolate look came over his face as he stared at the icy-cold water, and he went over to sit on the wall next to Lorenza. "*Margot me fout tout les temps,*" he said, dangling his hairy legs in the sun. "What?" Lorenza asked. "Oh, nothing. . . ."

Everybody took it for granted that he loved her; even Gregorio, the gardener, stopped to watch him as he cleaned the gravel in the

17

morning, rake in hand, expecting sooner or later to see some gesture of affection from Margot in response to such devotion.

But it was just as obvious that Margot didn't really care very much about his love. On the contrary, sometimes she acted as though she found it insufferable. I'm sick of it, sick of it! she would say all of a sudden. This was her territory, where she lorded it over everybody, not just that oversized boy with the glasses but also, besides the various suitors who showed up every day at Chesa Silvascina, Vivia and Marisetta. They were always ready to satisfy her every desire, to show enthusiasm for any proposal she might make, as if they saw the world through her eyes and it was only through her eyes that the world became "really fantastic." *Oh yes, let's do it* was one of their favorite expressions whenever Margot proposed an outing or a game of tennis. Or even just a walk as far as the lake.

Actually there were three lakes, separated by huge expanses of meadows with scattered old farmhouses and great big wooden barns. But for them there was only one lake, "*the* lake" that stretched as far as the Majola, changing from blue to an iron color, a lake that seemed to stretch out forever, almost grasping the mountains, fading into the sky in the evening twilight. A small island rose up in the middle of it, covered with larch and fir trees, where Alberto had gone one time with the sailboat, anchoring in the little sandy bay. But it was years ago now that the boat had been sold and nobody ever went out on the lake anymore, even though they talked about it as a familiar place. A place where you could go on moonlit winter nights when the lake was frozen over and covered with snow, and make a bonfire.

Every morning Signora Arnitz came down to check the flower beds alongside the house where the flowers were intermingled in all kinds of colors, still damp from the night. Signora Arnitz talked to herself and commented on their condition, her hands reaching into the spaces between one flower and another, trying to brush off some insect regarded as a menace, her short fat arms sticking out of the puffed sleeves of her dirndl. A dress which, in homage to some unspecified Bavarian ancestor, she seems to prefer for Chesa Silvascina; along with the big straw hat that protects her pink-white skin from the sun. The columbines, the flowers of the monkshood root, and those big, pale blue flowers of the thistle are, together with the petunias, her first thoughts in the morning, as though through the lightness of their petals she could somehow reach the poetry of the universe, taste the luminous wake left by Aurora's chariot, now gone from sight somewhere on the other side of Mt. Margna. For the little girl who has successfully struggled to finish her ovaltine all she has is a quick, critical glance. Not critical in the mean sense but in the sense of evaluation because with those stick-like legs and those shoulder blades poking up under her sweater, she brings her immediately back down to earth and the practical things of life. She always asks her if she had a good night, if she's still hungry, and if she's had enough to eat. She is kind, even though it's clear that the little girl means no more to her than Nelly, Gregorio's daughter. Lorenza always answers "yes" and watches as the shadow of her hat darkens the blue of her irises, small eyes as cold as pebbles. When she was young she *was involved in all kinds of escapades,* Marisetta says. But Lorenza can't imagine what kind of escapades she could possibly have been involved in with that look of the happy gardener, and to ingratiate herself she asks her the names of the flowers. "Eisenhüte," her grandmother says, "Alpenrosen," cutting here and there with the scissors with no apparent reason, in a way that seems slightly crazy, as if she wanted to save some flowers at the expense of others that were every bit as beautiful.

The mantelpiece in the living room is lined with photographs of her only son, Alberto, who died in Africa of a mysterious infection. A lot of them: Alberto as a child, Alberto on Mt. Bernina, Alberto at boarding school in Montreaux. Alberto on a sailboat. A boy with smooth, straight hair and intense eyes, perhaps of the same "veil of the Madonna" blue as hers. But the most beautiful photograph is in the hall, large and sharply contrasted, with the shadows etched dark against the majestic, snow-capped Mt. Corvatsch. Alberto is standing straight, in shirtsleeves, a wool knit vest his only protection against the cold on an afternoon where scattered wisps of clouds hover over the immaculate slope. His skis are planted crisscross in the snow behind him with their tips pointing up at the sky and Alberto wrinkles his brow just slightly to challenge the sun that strikes him in the face, his mouth half-open, a lock of hair blown upward by the wind against his forehead.

Marisetta is all that's left of him, born just before Alberto left for Africa. And it was in the Congo, going down the river following a snake hunter, that he had gotten that mysterious infection that was to eat his liver away, little by little. He had still wanted to go back there and it was there that he died, in a village made of straw and mud. But Marisetta, Nonna says, isn't at all like Alberto. She's lazy; indolent. At times she caresses her distractedly almost as if her fingers were searching her face for traces of that son of hers, vivacious and restless, always looking for new emotions. Marisetta smiles. She has a round, placid face, where pimples sprout suddenly during the night without altering her happy disposition. She knows from her mother that her father was violent and drank too much, and that it was because of the alcohol that his liver gave out. But she likes to stay with her Swiss Nonna, she says, with *Mamigna*, she quickly corrects herself (everyone has to call her Mamigna; Nonna must be too common) and every summer she arrives preceded by a small brass-studded trunk to spend her vacation time at Chesa Silvascina. Sometimes, when she leaves to go back to Milan, where her mother lives with her new husband, Chesa Silvascina has already seen its first snowfall.

But now it's been almost a year since another war has broken out. My God, it seems like yesterday that the Kaiser's war ended, Signora Arnitz says. It won't last long, let's hope, Germany is too strong, they've just been rolling over one army after another. But Marisetta, she adds, would do well not to leave Switzerland. She doesn't tell the little girl, however, that she too should stay on in the safety of Chesa Silvascina. Since that first test on the night she arrived she's never taken her hands again nor looked at her closely in the eye. The results had surely been negative: too dark, awkward. And then she takes so strikingly after that *nothing* of her father. She will do her duty and fatten her up with lots of milk, honey, and butter; and then, she's on her way, back home again.

Not even Vivia, Marisetta's inseparable friend, holds any interest for her. She's just a nice looking specimen that goes well with the garden and the house, neither more nor less than her pumped-up Persian cat with the round eyes sunk like glass into his fur. The truth is she likes having young people around. When Marisetta goes to tell her good night, she seems never to tire of hugging her tight, as Marisetta's eyes, languid with sleep, begin to close. She hugs Vivia too, though with less emotion; she even offers Eddy her cheek for a kiss and she runs her hand through his hair as if she wanted to keep his lips against her face just a little longer. And as they all leave the room she follows them with her gaze, listens to their footsteps going up the stairs, their voices and their laughter. The doors slamming shut.

With Margot she doesn't dare. Her favorite daughter doesn't like displays of emotion and she sighs and jokes about it. The little girl's "good night" is different; maybe because she hasn't been fattening up and always says yes without looking her in the eye. On some nights when Lorenza comes downstairs in her pajamas, looking for the book she's left behind, she finds her bent over the green tablecloth, her glasses down low on her nose and her uncombed crispy hair casting shadows over the blotches of color in the puzzle. She's always holding some small essential piece between her thumb and index finger ready to be put into place; without raising her eyes she tells her not to make noise, to go quietly up the stairs.

That old vampire, Lula the maid let it slip out once, exhausted from going up and down from one floor to the other, those girls that ring the bell even if it's only to have her bring them a glass of water or a sweater they've left up in their room. But if she complains that her legs ache from constantly climbing the stairs Signora Arnitz responds: what do you want, they're young. As if the word "young" were enough to justify laziness, arrogance, thoughtlessness.

Lorenza's hopes of becoming friends with Marisetta and Vivia have been dashed a while ago. She always just plays with Nelly, and maybe she has more fun. And yet in bed at night all she does is think about them and when she'll be grown up too and walk down the stairs at Chesa Silvascina with her long hair down to her shoulders, the taffeta of her skirt swishing at every step; and every time she hears the sound of the tires on the gravel she leans out the window to see Margot getting into the Bentley, Eddy walking around the car to open the door for her. If it's raining he holds the umbrella up high so she won't get wet, then he gets into the driver's seat and they're off to who knows where—to Silvaplana, to St. Moritz, where the big hotels are all lit up and all the young suitors crowd around Margot to ask her to dance.

It was as if she had to find some way to snatch Margot's magic formula from her, so that one day she could be exactly like her in everything and in every way: dressing, walking, laughing, throwing her hair back in that same way of hers, brash and yet apparently so natural that it always ends up concentrating everyone's attention on her. Something that sometimes creates annoyance and gives rise to sudden silences, jealousies. There are times when it seems that Vivia and Marisetta almost hate her. But when Margot goes away even for just a day, once they've gone wild making fun of Eddy or splashing around in the pool and tormenting Nonna's Persian cat,

22

they can't wait for her to come back. Shuffling around from room to room, their proud prancing reduced to an aimless trot from the house to the lawn, from the lawn to the house.

"You never say anything," she says, "It's a mistake to be so quiet all the time." It's a day of big clouds and the gray air blanches the skin on her high, wide cheekbones, slides across her forehead where her low hairline accentuates the roundness of her face. Who does she look like? Certainly not Nonna and not Mamma either. Her dark, thick eyelashes are what Lorenza envies most. She wants Lorenza to tell her about what she does when she's in Rome; to tell her about Marta and the games they play. She comes over to sit down beside her and her brown eyes that look like they've been dipped in honey stare at her, encouraging and seductive. Lorenza would love to let herself go and talk openly with her as she's seen Marisetta and Vivia do so many times. Talk about her sister and about the piano. But instead she answers stingily, with a sullen pout, as if she doesn't care. But even if that visit to her room is nothing more than a duty owed to the little girl who's always left to her own devices, Margot doesn't give up and now she starts talking to Lorenza about Mamma. Isabella, she calls her. She tells about how when she was little she felt a true adoration for her, even though they only saw each other in the summertime, when the older sister came home from boarding school. Unfortunately, Alberto was always around to mess things up, she adds quickly. When she came to Chesa Silvascina, Isabella didn't care about anyone else but him. Alberto, always Alberto. The two of them built a wall around themselves to keep everyone else away. And if Alberto did something wrong, Isabella was always ready to defend him, always, even when it was clear that he was wrong. Even when he drank and raised his voice. "Oh, how I hated him!" she says. But later on, when Alberto died in Africa and all that came back was a trunk with his books and the bottles of medicine, all those relief maps with the trails marked in red, oh, later on it was so terrible. . . . Mamigna just couldn't get over it and Isabella couldn't stand her, couldn't stand her scenes, her crying. . . . The friction between them started back then, she says. Isabella had become very religious and went to church every morning. Mamigna was even afraid she might join the convent.

"Mamma a nun?" Lorenza asked in shock. "That was just an idea of Mamigna's, I don't think Isabella ever considered it at all." She used to go with her to church a lot of times, she continues, she liked going out with her, and afterwards they would go together to get a pastry at Müller's. It was wonderful. Isabella had taught her how to say the Our Father and the Hail Mary, and even those ejaculations that you say to shorten your time in Purgatory; a hundred days of indulgence, three hundred. A year! And now Margot laughs, playing with Lorenza's fingers.

She took the photograph from the top of the dresser, the one where Isabella and Enrico are walking arm in arm along a tree-lined boulevard and Isabella is happy. She has a hat with a low brim down around her face, a short, knee-length skirt, Enrico holding her close to his side. "God, she's still so beautiful!" she says; but then her voice seems to tighten itself harshly around the words. Margot throws her hair back in that brash way her suitors find so attractive: "Is it possible she couldn't wait for me for even a day? That she couldn't even stay just one more night?" And all of a sudden she starts talking about when her sister had started criticizing everything she did. Nothing was good enough for her, not the way she dressed, the way she talked, not the friends she spent time with, not even the books she read. "And now what did she have to do that was so important?" She leaned down over the little girl as if she expected to be able to read the answer in her eyes. Hers have a darker circle around the iris now, a circle that makes them brighter but at the same time sets them off, as if all her thoughts were concentrated in that little honey-colored center: "What reason could she have to still be jealous of me?" To escape from that stare Lorenza concentrates on the metal buttons of her dress, the dirndl that she, like her mother, seems to prefer for Chesa Silvascina, and the only answer she offers is a shrug of her shoulders, her eyes fixed on the brown metal circles with the raised Alpine star. "Jealous?" she asks in a whisper. "Yes, jealous. That's something that happens between siblings, you know, just think about the story of Cain and Abel." Between her eyelashes the color of her eyes grows darker; maybe it's the day, maybe it's the rain that's started to draw lines on the windows, her gaze has something fixed about it together with something hard, the look of someone who has decided to challenge her adversary, certain of victory. Lorenza holds up even though she can feel her heart beating; "That's silly" she says in a low voice, "I'm not jealous of Marta at all."

Lorenza knows that Mamma can't stand her family; without distinctions. She also knows that Mamma has always thought that it was their fault that Alberto ended up dying in Africa. Maybe not Margot's. She was still a baby; but maybe hers too, yes. Exactly what fault Lorenza doesn't know, but "fault" was the word Mamma had used one time. Papà doesn't like them either, he always calls them snobs, completely devoid of culture. When Mamma decided she wanted to marry him, Nonna had said *not only is he from the South, but he's also a total nothing. . . .* Papà always joked about that "nothing". As if she, the *Semiramide*, were "something," he always adds, the daughter of that wine seller from the Valtellina who made all his money on those poor stonecutters from Como. . . .

That afternoon, the instant they heard Marisetta's voice on the stairs, Margot immediately left the room as if she had been waiting for an excuse to go. She turned away and disappeared with one of those quick, self-possessed movements that announce that something has ended; her stride that, despite the compactness of her body, looked so light she seemed to be gliding.

Neither she nor Lorenza could have known yet what was to happen one day at Chesa Silvascina, how the light can change from one minute to the next and turn the silk upholstery of a chaise longue into a lurid funeral shroud. Send the gray calm of an afternoon spinning into an inferno of noise. How thin the membrane is that separates one vision from another, similar one; and how the room with its window looking out toward Mt. Margna could one day be deformed into the place where acts and words would become *those* acts and *those* words. A place destined to close itself off in memory like a glass ball where the girl sitting on the bed is a skinny, haggard little imp and Margot a kind of film star, flashing into view here and there around the room like frames from an old movie (she would not return to Lorenza's room, despite the little girl's ardent hopes, ever again).

She appears at the window with her profile set against the gray of the clouds, her neck sticking out of the ruffles of her white cotton blouse. The dirndl doesn't become her. It's a doll's dress, and there's no doll in her. The dull light slithers across her hair to her forehead to reveal its post-suntan pallor, slightly mortuary. Her mouth, her cheekbones harden, sculpted by that unforgiving chalky reflection. Only her eyes, under the thin lines of her eyebrows, concentrate all of her seduction in their luminous pupils, determined to suck the little girl into the viscous circle of which she is the center; she doesn't know that the girl has already been trapped. Her voice, fresh and imperious as she says *what reason could she have to still be jealous of me* resonates like a bird call, a voice that cuts Lorenza to the quick because it seems to thrust her, her and Mamma, into the bottom of her miserable sack of petty jealousies. The rain outside the window weighs down on the branches of the larch trees and mingles with the low-lying smoke-like fog while Margot's white neck, too full for a nineteen-year-old girl, tilts just slightly to the side as she poses the question for which she already has the answer. Her hands, small and light with their thin fingertips, which she surely must have gotten from her aristocratic *viveur* father (Mamma and Nonna have big hands, white and slightly chubby) are still holding the photograph where Isabella and Enrico are walking arm in arm along the tree-lined boulevard at the moment the photographer said Stop! and, backing up a step, took their picture smiling among the luxuriant plane trees. But the instant that "Margot!" sounds on the stairs, the photograph suddenly loses all interest for her; she hurriedly puts it back in its place as the bright colors of her folksy dress are already vanishing on the other side of the door.

Beyond the road and the lawn, at the edge of the woods, was the chalet with the veranda where Gregorio piled the firewood. The squirrels went there to eat and every evening Nelly filled a bowl with hazelnuts for them. But it is also Margot's favorite place and she amuses herself with Marisetta and Vivia in its one big room cooking *würstel* and blood-rare steaks in the fireplace. Sometimes Nelly and Lorenza are invited to join in the fun too, and then it's a big party and they parade up and down with the plates and glasses; and to make the fiction seem real they steal Lula's apron. But most of the time the bigger girls tell them to go away and Nelly and Lorenza can hear them laughing, Eddy playing the harmonica while the smell of burning meat fills the air. The clamor of footsteps on the wood floor, who knows what they're up to; if they put their noses up to the windowpane they can see the fire in the fireplace and the glow of candlelight, and they're full of envy. But then Marisetta and Vivia close the curtains and they can't see anything. Suddenly they're alone as the darkness falls from the trees and the dry twigs snap under their feet. The rustling of some frightened animal running through the woods. And they run toward the house with their hearts in their throats and only when they've reached the front door, only then do they breathe a long sigh of relief.

But Signora Arnitz asks them immediately where they've come from, all panting and gasping for breath. In the morning, after she's finished with her flowers, she always sits in the living room with her books, the radio, and her enormous jigsaw puzzle. She rarely and reluctantly gets out of her armchair, slightly misshapen from her weight, keeping an eye on the movements in the house through the open door. When she hears footsteps she immediately asks who's there. Maybe she's upset not to know what Marisetta, Vivia, and Margot are doing at the moment. Or Eddy, the son of the man who had been her greatest love. Where have they gone? They never tell her. So she calls Lorenza while at the sound of her voice Nelly runs away, and the little girl has to tell her what she has seen or what she knows of *them* while Nonna looks at her with her lapis lazuli eyes. Lorenza stands there embarrassed, feeling like she's playing the spy, but at the same time she feels important and wants to give her all the information she desires. Maybe even make something up. She knows she should be grateful for Nonna's hospitality, and as her father said, *she's giving her the opportunity to get over all those annoying little fevers that keep her from growing up strong and happy like Marta*. In exchange for such kindness, maybe Nonna expects her to make herself useful somehow; and so she tells her what she has seen and also what she hasn't seen, her feet rubbing up against each other in her embarrassment, getting dirt on the beautiful Turkish carpet.

On cooler days the fireplace in the living room is lit but Lorenza and the older girls are not allowed to warm up near it because Signora Arnitz wants them to get used to the cold. Otherwise how will they be able to stand it when they go to dances in low cut dresses, those dances in those old salons that no radiator is able to heat? Lorenza doesn't believe she'll ever go to parties like that; and when Nonna isn't looking, she puts her hands up close to the fire while her eyes look up at the mantel and the photographs of Alberto, in a progression that goes from the child with his beret to the bare-chested young man on the bow of a boat. Leaning up against his shoulder a young woman smiles, her bathing suit leaving her stomach bare—a bathing suit which is certainly very daring. Was Alberto a *viveur* too?

Nelly has told her that Signora Arnitz's second husband was a *viveur* and that the Signora had thrown him out of the house. "He was what?" Lorenza asked. "A *viveur*," Nelly insists. She is almost two years older than Lorenza but she doesn't know how to explain what *viveur* means and she tells how afterward he had found a new wife and how one day he had gone to America and they'd never heard from him again. He didn't even keep in touch with Margot, his daughter. When he used to come to Chesa Silvascina, she says, if Signora Arnitz went away, he always brought some women in and the fireplace would go all night long. "What women?" Lorenza asked. "Just some women" Nelly repeated. And then Lorenza laughs scornfully because she thinks what Nelly has told her is really stupid. But Nelly insists, saying that they were women who danced naked on trays of sweets. At that point Lorenza starts laughing even louder and mimics the disjointed gestures of a dancing marionette.

But her time is coming to an end. Papà has written to say that he will come to pick her up and to ask if someone can accompany her as far as Chiavenna. Eddy will go with her, Nonna says, he'll accompany her in the Bentley. Meanwhile the Bentley is always in the garage under Gregorio's apartment. Hardly anybody uses it anymore because of the shortage of gasoline coupons.

It's a very bright afternoon; the sunlight, in a prelude to September, meanders along, chasing the shadows, promising a perfect sunset. At the end of the lawn the larch trees are rubbing their large pointed limbs together and Lorenza is sitting on a canvas folding chair, her head bent over a book. But the adventures of *Bibi, a Girl from the North*, are too distant, they've got nothing in common with her scant and limited experience, and her loneliness fades into the cardboard blue sky. Rare, small clouds fly by in frayed, wispy white. The air stings but the grass is still warm and the bees are making the monkshood flutter. *They* are over there, their bodies flexing toward the water in the pool where some solitary insect floats along, pulled by the slight current. Nobody goes in swimming anymore. Eddy is taking pictures of them; he's always taking pictures of everything. The girls tell him no, they've had enough, and their hands fly up like doves to cover their faces. Then Margot goes over to sit on the grass next to the table where Lula has put the big stout teapot. She has a man's jacket over her shoulders. Maybe it's Eddy's, or maybe it belongs to the suitor who's drinking from a cup with light blue designs on it. Lorenza is upset with her because of those things she said about her mother, because she acts like nothing is important in the world except her way of laughing or getting angry. Or her way of crying, like that time she didn't want them to kill the marmot. She wanted to nurse it back to health and she screamed and cried, and the only living things in the world were she and her marmot, who was more dead than alive; and Gregorio was right to want to put it out of its misery with a blow of his shovel.

The suitor has his hair slicked back with brilliantine (he obviously keeps it under a wide-mesh cotton net at night) and his cheeks are slightly puffed out as though he always keeps a piece of candy in his mouth. He seems to be very intelligent and his university thesis has already been placed on the examining commission's table, to the wonder of his professors. His lips are pink and get all wet with saliva when he talks, his long-fingered hand with the protruding veins passes over them quickly to dry it. He meets with the decided approval of Signora Arnitz, who praises his elegance and his gentlemanly self-assurance, and pours some more tea into his cup. Even Margot seems not to disdain him and, sitting on the grass with her arms hugging her bare knees, she lifts her face to listen. She is Margot the *daughter of daughters*, destined to dedicate herself completely and totally to the service of her mother's plans, which vaguely contemplate something extraordinary for her. The young man's moist and slightly puffy lips close around the rim of his cup. "Pétain," he says between sips, "Pétain knew quite well what he was up against, and now we'll see what kind of new constitution he's capable of inventing with the Germans at his back. . . ." Margot's eyebrows contract in concentration; but then Eddy leans over her and whispers something the others are not supposed to hear as the Kodak dangling from his neck brushes against her cheek. Eddy is too young, Signora Arnitz always says, and besides he's not very healthy. Eddy is big, clumsy, but Margot's eyes stare at his mouth as though a little procession of angels were about to stream out of it. He laughs and now maybe he mutters some ironic comment at the expense of that know-it-all suitor and Margot pushes him away roughly: "Stop it," she says, "I want to listen." She doesn't want to miss a word of what the suitor has to say about the 25 June speech of President Pilet Golaz, a speech that Mamigna liked so much. "It was a national digrace," he says, "It was a Nazi speech that accepted a German victory . . ." Even though he comes from the canton of Zurich, he speaks almost perfect Italian, the cadence is just a little slower, the r farther back in the throat. "But that's how it is; it's as if they've already won," Signora Arnitz says. "That's not true," he replies, "England's army is still almost intact and its navy is the strongest in the world; and behind England there's America, there's Roosevelt." "But if even the Italians have succeeded in invading British Somaliland!" Signora Arnitz interrupted him. "Oh, the Italians . . . they're exactly what in German are called *Schnorrer!*"

Signora Arnitz is left holding the raised teapot in her hand. A teapot, like the cups, made of Danish porcelain; she loves everything that comes from the North and so little of what comes from the South. But now that excessively brutal reference to her country of origin has offended her. "Somalia," she says, clipping her words, "belongs to the Italians by right." "What right? Everybody talks about rights but even we have forgotten that there exists a right of asylum, and we continue to send away all the refugees that arrive at our borders. That "J" that's being used to earmark the passports of Jews is horrifying."

Oh, the right of asylum, all this talk about the right of asylum . . . Signora Arnitz watches the milk expand like a small cloud in her teacup, but who will defend their rights if Hitler gets it in his head to come and take them back, the Jews? Who? Stalin maybe? Mussolini? Or maybe General Guisan. Would you really like to see what our General Guisan could do, with all of his good intentions, against the Panzerdivisionen. . . .

"What are you talking about?" Margot is on her feet, "Nobody is threatening us." The light filtering through the larch trees falls on the *Journal de Genève* and the *Nationalzeitung* and a light breeze turns the pages of the magazine left sitting on the grass. The shadows come and go over Hitler and Mussolini shaking hands, their brown and greenish gray uniforms there on the page a lighter gray and a darker gray, almost black. "Please dear," Signora Arnitz has raised her voice to address the little girl sitting on the canvas folding chair, "go tell Lula to bring the cake." She doesn't want to argue with Margot in front of her favorite suitor, doesn't want to disturb that idyllic afternoon respite: tea, youth, family. Margot and the pink-lipped suitor look at each other, "I'm cold," she says, "I'm going in to get a sweater" and the splendor of the afternoon seems to dissolve on the golden skin of her face, raise with a slight chill the fair hair on her arms. She gets up and stretches, yawns. Standing on the grass she looks like a clown in that jacket that's too big and too long for her, and she smiles as if to excuse herself for that stretch and that yawn. "You want to come with me?" she asks the suitor, still sitting across from her mother. She throws the jacket that's not hers over a chair and seems suddenly to have made a choice. All she needs to forget about General Guisan, British Somaliland, is the walnut cake that the cook has just taken out of the oven. Even Signora Arnitz and Eddy are small and insignificant there on the grass as the two of them head toward the house, the dust they raise illuminating them among the afternoon shadows. On their way they go right past the little girl who is on her way inside to call Lula. They don't even seem to notice her, as an oily wake of brilliantine follows in their footsteps.

"We're a family of liberals," Signora Arnitz always says. She likes to recall her grandfather who emigrated to Canton Ticino in August of 1849 when the Austrians took back Milan; and she is disappointed now not to be able to continue her discussion with the young man who studies political economy and who surely will become a minister or something of that sort. But by now they are all tired of important discussions and only Lorenza is still sitting there in front of her grandmother waiting for the knife to sink into the cake dusted with powdered sugar. Eddy has gone too, to join Vivia and Marisetta for a game of rummy; but before he left he took one last picture and the Kodak opened and closed its eye to capture Signora Arnitz and the little girl. Lula standing on the grass with her apron strings knotted at the waist. The light and shadows of that wondrous afternoon. One of the few without so much as a cloud in that rainy August of 1940.

The next day the weather changed again and Marisetta stayed in bed all day with a fever. It was still raining that evening and when Nelly and Lorenza went out to take some hazelnuts to the squirrels there was a big umbrella left dripping outside the chalet. It was already late and there was no light coming from the two little windows. They pushed on the door that had been left ajar and as soon as their eyes were used to the dark some dirty plates appeared on the floor, apple peels, pieces of cookies scattered all around together with cigarette butts. A half-full bottle of wine was sitting next to some pillows piled up on the floor in front of the fireplace where the embers barely glowed in the dark. Who had made such a mess in the chalet? Marisetta had spent the whole day in bed and

33

Vivia and Margot had gone out right after lunch with Eddy to go to the movies in St. Mortiz. Who then? The girls ran back out through the rain to look for Gregorio, but Gregorio wasn't there and so they went back into the house, panting, the water pouring down off their rubber ponchos.

Signora Arnitz was reading and the light from the lamp shone on her dull, crispy hair. Gasping for breath, Lorenza told her that someone, maybe some burglars, had gone into the chalet and messed it all up. Signora Arnitz took off her glasses, "Explain what you mean," she said. She didn't seem at all surprised or frightened and her eyes were pointed at her like two little daggers. So Lorenza described what she had seen as Nonna's face slowly changed expression, losing that pink-white color that she protected so carefully. Lorenza was swallowing her saliva from the emotion and she could see Nelly outside the open door stretching her neck to listen, her braids like two wet tails. Maybe they weren't robbers, she corrected herself, but some gypsies who went in there to take shelter from the rain.

"Don't be silly. There aren't any gypsies around here." Nonna was looking at her trying to understand how much of it was true and how much she was making up. Then Lorenza told her about the pillows on the floor, as if someone had slept on them. "Go call Lula," Nonna said; and as soon as Lula came in Signora Arnitz ordered her to go put the chalet back in order. "It's late now; it's dark," the maid protested. "Take Gregorio out there with you." She was furious and little red veins had popped out all over her face. But as soon as they were outside the living room, Lula started in on the little girl. Why had she gone nosing around in the chalet? Why didn't she mind her own business and leave everybody else in peace? She cut herself off immediately, however, when Signora Arnitz appeared at the door, her glasses still on her nose, and shouted up the stairs to Vivia.

34

"It's all Margot's fault." Vivia was crying and her shiny brown hair was down over her face like a veil. The only innocent one seemed to be Marisetta who had stayed in bed all day and was now trying to console her friend, lending her a handkerchief. "I want to leave," Vivia said, "That's it; I want to go home. This time I don't have anything to do with it, ask Eddy." But Eddy was nowhere to be found; his raincoat was still hanging on the hook in the entryway and nobody knew where he had gone in all that rain while Margot, who had just come home, was sitting on the little table in the bathroom, cutting her nails, indifferent to all the agitation.

That evening, when the gong sounded to call everyone to the dinner table, Eddy's place remained empty. Vivia's eyes were still red and she still hadn't stopped sniffling. "How long are you going to keep this up?" Margot said. She was flushed and her round chin stuck out along with her cheekbones under the antler-shaped lamp. She seemed especially animated and kept talking between bites; but she was more thirsty than hungry and kept asking for great big glasses of water that she drank down in a single swallow. Only her hands, busily tearing up pieces of bread on the tablecloth, fretful little mouse paws, betrayed her agitation.

Signora Arnitz hadn't come down to dinner. The living room was dark and through the open door you could see the last flames of the fire flickering in the fireplace. Lorenza didn't dare ask any questions and kept her head low as she conscientiously ate everything Lula put on her plate. "Don't just sit there pouting," Margot said suddenly, "Nothing's wrong, and anyway it's not your fault," and she smiled at her from the other end of the table, offering her another piece of cake.

When Eddy came in they were already folding up their napkins. He was drenched from head to foot, his hair dripping in his eyes. "Is there any strudel left for me?" he asked. He wasn't wearing his glasses and batted his eyelids, his skewed eye like a crazed wing on his pallid face. "Go change your clothes," Margot told him, "otherwise you'll catch pneumonia," and then in that fast, incomprehensible lingo of theirs, she said something to him about Mamigna and her fury.

A fury that was unleashed against Margot later that evening. Behind the closed door you could hear her voice, low and hesitant, a voice that dwindled slowly into silence under the steady onslaught from the voice of her mother; acute, harsh, and plaintive at the same time—almost crying. Was Mamigna crying or was she faking it? "Be serious," said Marisetta, hurrying back into bed, "She doesn't even know what tears are, but why doesn't she leave them alone, those two?" The voices kept on for a long time, with highs and lows, and while she was brushing her teeth Lorenza heard a great slamming of doors and Eddy running up the stairs where the girls' rooms were. In the mirror above the sink she looked at her oversized flannel pajamas, shapeless on her graceless body, the toothpaste dripping slowly down the side of her mouth, mixed with saliva. Something had gone over her head, had flown by without her even noticing it, and now she could hear its long screech, like the sound of a bat. Something that involved everybody except her and Nelly. And now just like Vivia, she was overcome by a violent desire to get away from there, to go back home. She didn't care at all anymore about the room papered with white canvas and foliage, about the yellow silk chaise longue where she could stretch out like a princess, or the big tub she sank into so happily, opening and closing the faucet to watch the water gush out from the jaws of the lion. She wanted to go home, right away; and if she hadn't been so afraid of the dark, she would have run out into the rain to look for a telephone to call Mamma.

Papà, Marta, Mamma. But Marta isn't there, she stayed at home with Aldina, Papà says. Marta is still too little to take such a long trip Mamma adds; and Lorenza is glad she's not there because this way she'll have the two of them all to herself. She saw them from the Bentley as they sat at an outside table at the café. She could see her mother's back with its slight bulge up high near her neck and her hat angled down over her curls. She could see her shoes with the blue shoelaces, those shoes that have something magic about them because she only wears them to get on and off trains. To walk along the platform in and out of puffs of steam behind the porter with the bags, her heels beating like little hammers against the pavement.

Eddy greeted them, sticking his head out the car window as Lorenza jumped out even before he pulled on the brake. Papà stood up immediately: he's tall, balding at the temples, and the little girl adores his lean body when she hugs him. His fragility is only apparent, because when it comes to lifting a suitcase no one does it as easily as he does. Lorenza feels like crying for joy in his arms but she knows that Papà would be frightened, he gets alarmed by tears and doesn't like them. So she kisses him on the nose, just like Papà always does with her, sucking on it just a little. Like a good Swiss lady, Mamma takes care to maintain a dignified demeanor in front of Eddy and pats the little girl's hair back into place after her impetuous exit from the car. The air is heavy and gray, and there's no wind at all. It's starting to get dark and Papà has offered Eddy a glass of vermouth. Lorenza has ordered an orangeade, sipping it through a straw. They talk about the war that has begun in Italy in the past few months. Eddy says that this is probably the last trip he'll take in the Bentley because since the advance of the Italian troops in Africa, gasoline has been harder and harder to find. Mamma tells him how happy she is to see Lorenza looking so well, the color in her cheeks. She seems like a different person, she says; and Papà wants to take her to the pharmacy right then and there to check on the scale how much weight she has gained. Mamma asks Eddy how much longer they plan to stay on at Chesa Silvascina. Eddy doesn't know, after what's happened, the war and all the rest of it, he doesn't know. "But you'll all be fine just the same wherever you are, why should you be worried?" Mamma asks him. "You never know, with all these refugees coming from all over the place. Mamigna is worried and she doesn't want to go to Lugano." At the word *Mamigna*, Papà's face breaks into an ironic smile, his crossed leg bobbing up and down impatiently. "Isabella," he interrupts them, "maybe we should be going; we'll miss our train." Eddy and Mamma give each other a kiss and as she moves her cheek up to his mouth, there seems to be some resemblance between them. In the cut of their eyes, in their pale, slightly rounded foreheads. Or maybe it's their complexion, very fair and quick to blush. Papà has the bags loaded on a cart and Eddy shakes Lorenza's hand, a strong grip like the first night she arrived at Chesa Silvascina. Lorenza watches him get back in the Bentley and turn around to head out on the return trip, the back of his neck with the closely cropped hair standing out clearly in the dark. And just like that, as the car disappears into the darkness between the mountains, she is overcome with a feeling of nostalgia, a sense of loss. Everything that had amazed her and shocked her in those two months at Chesa Silvascina, that had fascinated her and filled her with wonder, *their* voices and *their* lingo, even the jealousy and the loneliness, has suddenly turned into a sense of suffocation, almost panic. Something that was hers, that had been hers, and was now once again only *theirs*.

3

He was there again on the landing, waiting with a jacket over a pea green sweater and his hands in his pockets. As soon as she saw him from the peephole in the service door, Lorenza ran to the entryway to have him admire what little new meat she'd put on her bones with the bread and butter and the strudel, and Mamigna's walnut cake.

But Mamma got there first. Arturo reeks of tobacco and Isabella is all that exists for him, Isabella with her hand still on the door handle and her myopic eyes bursting with joy. And as they embrace she leans her head on his shoulder as if she wanted to laugh and cry at the same time: she's almost as tall as Arturo but suddenly she seems small, defenseless, the strong curves of her body pressed up against his, as if they've turned to rubber. Instinctively, Lorenza has removed herself from the scene; the universe Mamma-Arturo-Papà has turned upside down, and she's been thrown to the ground, struck by lightning like Saint Paul. The little girl who spied on them from the opening in the door behind the piano has left her place to another girl for whom the months spent at Chesa Silvascina have opened new horizons; and now she feels relegated to some faraway and imprecise point in the firmament. A point utterly without significance. That little bit of new meat on her bones, hard won in the digestion of long and elaborate meals, the cold air stinging her cheeks, no longer matters at all. The little girl that Arturo used to call "my little bag of bones" has lost her shine, doesn't count for anything anymore. Only Mamma, big and blond (too fat, too fat) who shows her love without restraint, only she exists, warmed by that embrace, which unfolds ever so slowly as each word, even the most banal, catches fire in their eyes.

They're all together around the table again and Arturo is joking with the children; or at least he is trying to, like he used to do, with that carefree, boyish talk of his. But Lorenza resists, chewing slowly and tenaciously, and looks over at Papà, waiting for him to unleash his sword and become the avenging angel. Impatient she waits for him to cut his meat, holding it still with his fork, then his pallid hand closes around the wine glass; he breaks a bread stick and talks about what's happened during Arturo's absence, about the shameful removal of Tullio Levi-Civita from the editorial board of *Zentralblatt*. And now, he says, the *Mathematical Review*, which is published in the United States, has outclassed the German journal and they've been left out in the cold. Instead of transfixing Arturo with his sword he goes on at length about the vacuum created in the department by the loss of professors like Ascoli, Bemporad, Enriques, his knife and fork inert on the plate, his cutlet still almost intact, with no sign of alarm in his gestures, in those distant eyes behind his glasses, about the way those two are looking at each other. About the little girl's wrathful heart, beating against the side of the table. And in zoology, he continues, the director of the institute, Zavattari, besides that lovely gesture of signing the Manifesto of the Racial Scientists, has started promoting a course in genetics and the biology of race!

"That's enough," Arturo has interrupted him, "Let's stop torturing Isabella." Isabella is chewing slowly, a tiny piece of salad caught between her teeth. "It's true," she says, "it's been torture. Constant, relentless torture. It's been going on like this for months," her fingers collecting the crumbs on the tablecloth and then spreading them around again. "But you needn't be too worried about me," Arturo reaches out his hand as if he wanted to stop those restless fingers, "As far as I'm concerned, things have been going fine. In

Paris I was able to work in peace; it's been years since I was able to do that. And I also heard some wonderful music." God, his love for Isabella is so obvious now, his hand has almost reached her fingers, then it stops suddenly. Dark. Nervous. Is it possible that *he* doesn't notice?

Aldina comes and goes from the kitchen, Marta stares ecstatically at Mamma, for her Mamma's every word is a perfect circle where the *r*s skip along like baby goats and the *s*s are long and thin as needles. But Lorenza is just waiting for Papà to bring down his sword, and *z-z-zak*, with one clean blow, cut the thread that those two are stretching out to each other across the white tablecloth, a tablecloth that Isabella insisted on spreading on the table herself. And then she put on the plates with the gold striped border, and the wine goblets they used for festive occasions. "Several times I had the good fortune of hearing Milstein," Arturo is saying now, "he played some of Bach's partitas for violin — unforgettable." Now listen, Arturo, there's a surprise for you; Isabella smiles, that tiny unnoticed piece of salad ruining all that perfection. But Aldina has begun to change the plates, letting the knives and forks fall noisily against the porcelain, seemingly on purpose, and now she's complaining because Marta hasn't finished her meat. She, Isabella, doesn't bat an eyelash; who cares about Aldina, Marta, the vulgarity of food? "Did he play the partita *en ré mineur*?" she asks (oh, her odious French!). Arturo looks at her astonished; she laughs, extending the palms of her hands as if she were offering everyone an invisible gift, her eyes transparent as aquamarines, totally unrestrained.

But at last the Frog Prince has woken up from his torpor and jumped up on the table to ruin the surprise. "Since you left" he says, "Isabella has been forced to develop a taste for music," his hand reaching out to grasp his wife's, his chin speckled with a few little spots of gravy. "Is that so? Splendid!" Arturo shows his incredulity. Maybe he's faking it, but there's certainly none of the joy in his astonishment that she was expecting. "Try and try again, and

41

in the end you will succeed," Enrico's voice has just a barely perceptible tone of triumph as his fingers tighten around those of his wife. "Oh, it wasn't all that difficult," she protests. "I wonder if now you finally understand our unbridled passion for Bach," Arturo's glance skims over those white fingers abandoned in Enrico's grip, "a passion that sometimes has a touch of dementia, like for that slow variation on the chaconne, with that almost choral effect." "The chaconne, in the second movement?" "But no, the chaconne is the last, after the gigue!" Enrico interrupts her. "Oh, that's right." Her eyelids have that imperceptible tremor they get when something embarrasses her, but Enrico is already talking over her voice. "I, however, still prefer the opening notes of the allemande," he says, turning to Arturo, "so similar to the beginning of the suite in G minor for piano, even though I must admit there's something magical about those three notes that keep returning in the chaconne." She can't keep up with them now and she and Arturo have stopped looking at each other; they've undoubtedly dared too much and now the light sound of the tangerine seeds that the girls are spitting into their plates blends with the phrases meant to exclude her. *No prelude*—they say—*free chords . . . descending*—those fingers still there in Enrico's grip as if forgotten. *That four-beat theme until it breaks into D major . . .* The voice that hums the motif is clear, agile, just a litle bit sharp. *And then those three repeated notes only in the high part and then again later on in the low part, like an echo.* A walnut cracks in the vise of the nutcracker, shell fragments spraying onto the carpet. Isabella's attention has shifted to the girls. She has slowly slipped her hand free from her husband's to peel an apple for Marta and now the squeal of the tram rounding the curve drowns out Arturo's voice, and Enrico's, who has gotten up to rummage through the programs kept in such neat order on the piano. "I can't remember now who played it the last time," he says, "A concert that was absolutely disappointing," and the oblique autumn sun strikes the water pitcher, the half-full

42

glasses, as the program sheets scatter into disorder on the mahogany shelf. Marta stares at Mamma's fingers as they guide the knife around the apple; the peel must remain in one piece, like a ribbon. Afterward Marta winds it back together and offers it to Aldina as though it were a real apple. And Aldina pretends to fall for it every time.

They've started going out again, the three of them together, and Mamma has a new silk scarf that Arturo has brought her from France. But it's not the same anymore, they stay out for hours, Enrico skips his lessons at the university and Isabella forgets to check over the girls' homework, to make sure they take a bath and that they wash behind their ears.

Arturo shows up at unthinkable hours and in the kitchen Aldina complains because even though she's already mopped the floor she has to put the water on again for pasta or make an omelet. "Why should I have to wait on that guy," she mutters bitterly, shuffling around the still wet floor, "I shouldn't even let him in the door." And she looks askance at the girls too; they feel ashamed for Mamma and even more for Papà who doesn't say a word and allows Aldina to be *forced into serving that guy*. And when Arturo comes they're not allowed to eat with him anymore. Children mustn't hear certain things because then they'd repeat them outside. All children have to think about is doing their homework and studying for tomorrow's lesson; and when they've finished maybe they can read a good book. There are some wonderful ones here, Papà says, pulling them down off the shelves in the entryway, "No use wasting time."

At home, when Arturo's not there, Mamma and Papà often talk about him, about "his difficulties." Arturo doesn't want to go back to France, they say, now that the Fascists are in control there too. But he can't live in Italy anymore. He's right, Papà says, how can you live when you're not allowed to do anything, not only to teach and study, but to have a telephone, a radio, to go to the cinema or walk into a café. Or even take the tram, or ride an elevator. For someone like him, who hates putting up with any limitations, every prohibition turns into a torment; and with each new restriction there's a greater risk of being taken for a subversive.

His jackets are more threadbare all the time; his raincoat got a big hole in it and Isabella has mended it. Badly; but Arturo doesn't care about having a jacket so worn the lining shows through at the elbows, or a beggar's raincoat, and he comes by almost every day, wearing out what's left of the soles on his shoes, his raincoat flapping in the wind.

If it hadn't been for his mother, who was very sick, he would have gone to the United States a while ago, Papà says. And there he might even have become a real scientist, one of the great ones. It's only because he didn't want to leave her alone that he didn't emigrate when it was time. But the older of the two girls thinks that if Arturo hasn't shared the same fate as professors like Bemporad and Enriques, it's not only because of his mother, who ended up dying; and she secretly observes the glances between Arturo and Isabella, pauses silently in the hall to listen to what the two of them are saying in the entryway. Such curiosity is a sin, her confessor has told her, your mother is your mother. She's sacred.

One day she saw them sitting at a café in Piazza del Popolo, a café where Arturo always used to go, *before*. He was wearing that mended raincoat of his and Isabella was turning her cup around in her hands, her lavender silk scarf abandoned on the chair. Arturo was holding some papers and was explaining something to her; she kept looking around as if she were afraid. Afraid that Arturo would be sent away, afraid for herself, that someone would see her? Lorenza can't quite understand. Mamma is facing away from her, and, looking through the glass, she tries to figure out where their hands are, their knees, if there's something *hidden* between them. Mamma nods her head to say "yes" and then suddenly covers her face, those blond curls slipping through her fingers. Her blue overcoat is unbuttoned and her soft breasts, cradled in the wool of her dress, brush up against the edge of the table. "But that's Arturo," Marta says. "Don't be so stupid," Lorenza scolds her, "You're not supposed to stare at people like that." But Marta has recognized Mamma and wants to run inside, surprise her, give her a hug. Just then Aldina comes out of the bakery with the bag of bread. "We can't," Lorenza says, rushing to drag her away by her sleeve. "We can't. Arturo is Jewish."

After that, everything took place on a stage where the girls were not present. It wasn't until many years later, when it was all long since over and done with, that Lorenza would try to retrace their footsteps, their gestures, their words, as if by touching her during that brief period of her life, they had contaminated her, and a part of them had gotten into her blood.

That winter, when Arturo left again, it was forever. Lorenza had seen him for the last time while she was waiting for the elevator in the foyer after coming home from school. Arturo was coming down the stairs with Mamma. It was cold and he was wearing a gray felt hat high up on his forehead. Mamma had on her three-quarter-length beaver coat and her hair was hidden under a knit wool turban. In response to some premonition Lorenza looked at her shoes to see if they were the ones with the blue ribbons, her "traveling shoes," but she was wearing galoshes and her shoes were covered. Her galoshes came down the stairs without a sound and Arturo's steps didn't seem to make any noise either. When Aldina opened the door for her, Lorenza immediately ran in to see how many places were set at the table. Papà was sitting in his reclining chair near the radio; he had taken off his jacket to put on his camel-hair sweater and was reading the newspaper while Marta, who had not gone to school that morning, was playing with the keys of the piano, which had been left open. Only three places were set. "Has Marta already eaten?" she asked, her throat tight to keep from crying. "No, no, I haven't eaten anything yet," her sister protested, and stopped hitting the piano to look at her as if she had to defend her rights. "It's just me, you, and Marta. Mamma's not home," Papà turned the page of his newspaper without even looking up. "Go wash your hands; it's ready," he added, his glasses shining in the dull light of the colorless day. Marta closed the piano with a bang and the urge to cry overwhelmed Lorenza, took control of her lungs, her legs, her arms, as her book bag fell from her hands and dropped to the floor. Finally her sobs forced Papà to take his eyes off the newspaper. Heartbreaking sobs. But Papà, as Lorenza knows all too well, doesn't like tears. "Now then, what are you doing? Why are you crying, you silly thing?" Lorenza threw herself into his arms. "Mamma's gone away," she said, between one sob an another, "she's gone away with Arturo," her tears streaming down on the wool of his sweater and the leather buttons shaped like little soccer balls sinking painfully into her cheek. "What are you talking about?" Papà's voice is irritated; he sets the child down, trying to put the crumpled up newspaper back in order, "She's gone to accompany him to the Swiss embassy." Then he feels sorry for her, "Come on now, go wash your hands, and your face too." He doesn't look at her, his thin, pale nose sticking out from the regular features of his handsome face, "When you've calmed down, we'll have a little talk together."

But then Aldina came in with a plateful of gnocchi and they sat down at the table, unfolding their napkins. Outside the windows the flat gray day was coming hopelessly to a close among the travertine apartment buildings and the sharp squeal of the tram rattling into the distance along Via Flaminia. "Professor Cohen says goodbye, he's gone away," Papà said to Aldina. "Has he already left?" she asked, showing her surprise. "He's leaving today, or tomorrow." "Cohen," Marta repeated as Aldina tied her napkin behind her neck, "That's the name of the store where Mamma bought me my overcoat." "It's not called that anymore," Lorenza corrects her,

46

"They've changed the name." The gnocchi are too hot and Marta has spread them around on her plate; *Cohen*, she repeats, as if she has discovered the magic word that might bring a ray of light into the otherwise dull day. "Enough now," Aldina says, stopping that fork that's spreading the gnocchi all over the plate, "Eat before they get cold." Marta is her favorite and she slips onto her plate another piece of the top crust, where the butter has formed some little brown bubbles. "According to the state of Italy," Papà tries to explain meanwhile, "Arturo is Jewish, even though only his father was Jewish and he doesn't practice his religion. But he's considered a Jew all the same because his mother was half French and half Romanian, a foreigner in other words. But in France, Vichy France, those who have only one Jewish parent and who don't practice their religion aren't considered Jews. That's why Arturo might be able to go back there to work. But he doesn't want to go live with another bunch of Fascists, like the ones in power in Vichy right now, and today he was going to make one last attempt to go to Switzerland. Mamma has gone with him to the Swiss embassy in the hope of getting him an entry visa. Although I don't think there's anything she can do."

The girls haven't understood a thing but they're hungry. Aldina has been left holding the plate in her hand. She hasn't understood much either but she asks, "Why?" "Why what?" "Why that thing about Vichy, there yes and here no?" "What do I know," Papà answered, "Ask that genius Mussolini."

4

It was many years later, when the war was long over, that Lorenza went back to Chesa Silvascina. The house had been sold and transformed into a pension with geraniums in the windows, and from the gravel patio, through the vestibule that had once served as a storage area for skis, one now arrived at the reception desk with room keys hanging from their hooks. Elderly Swiss couples sat in the garden and a pair of colored umbrellas were arranged on the lawn along with some clear-varnished tables. The red flag with the white cross waved from the balcony of what used to be Marisetta's room, and water still flowed in and out of the pool, ice-cold and clean. But the flagstone bottom was covered with a dark layer of moss, and the shrubs around the pool had grown, partially covering the stones along the edge. Green and gray, swaying in the wind, they skimmed the surface of the water while some insect floated along, like long ago, struggling sporadically to keep from being dragged away by the invisible current.

She didn't go into the house. She asked a few questions of the woman who ran the pension, who told her that the interior hadn't been changed. All they had done was add bathrooms, inserting them like so many cubes, in the rooms on the top floor, the ones that used to be the servants' quarters. Earnest and pleasant, she gave an impression of great solidity and the flowers that grew in the flower beds along the side of the house were tall and vigorous, water droplets shining on their petals. Her guests seemed to feel at home and when she told them that the visiting lady had lived in the house when it was still *ein Familienhaus*, they showed polite disinterest. They spoke German and only one or two of them knew a few words of Italian. Even the carriage house where Gregorio had lived above the garage and the Bentley was still the same. Now she, the owner, lived there and her husband watered the old red currant bushes with a long green plastic hose. The rates at the pension are not high, she said later on with her self-assured smile, but it was necessary to reserve several months in advance because there weren't many rooms and there was a big demand. "The place is quite popular," she added with a certain satisfaction, and wanted to at least show her the dining room. "Another time," Lorenza replied, thanking her.

Nor did she go out as far as the chalet at the edge of the woods. It was all overgrown and the wood siding was falling apart; the only thing still intact was the bowl that Nelly had filled every evening with hazelnuts for the squirrels.

The first to leave Chesa Silvascina were Gregorio and his family, in June of '43. An uncle had left him a small inheritance and Gregorio decided to open a pastry shop in Mendrisio. The morning of the move, as the cart waited on the road for the last boxes to be loaded, no one was home at Chesa Silvascina and the shutters were shut tight. Squirrels scampered undisturbed up and down the tree trunks, venturing out on the lawn with their tails curled behind them. Nelly chased after the little roe deer one last time when he appeared on the edge of the woods, and the telephone, which had just been installed a month ago, rang and rang in the dark vestibule under the photo of Alberto on Mt. Corvatsch. But when Gregorio ran to answer it nobody was there. Later it was learned that it was Marisetta who had called to see if her grandmother had come back yet from her therapy in Link, in the hills above Bern.

Gregorio was replaced by a custodian from Unterwalden who spoke German and mowed the lawn in a leather apron. Geraniums appeared in the windows of the carriage house and some red currant bushes were planted nearby. In May, General von Arnim had surrendered to the English army in Africa and the Germans multiplied the pillboxes along the windblown beaches of the Atlantic in preparation for what appeared to be an imminent invasion. The Swiss border with France was closed and General Guisan deployed his troops to block the entry of additional refugees. Especially Jews. After November '42 when the German armored divisions had occupied what had been the so-called *free zone of Vichy*, the Jews had no other escape route except for Switzerland and the small strip of Upper Savoy still occupied by the Italians.

As was her annual custom, the *gnädige Frau* (as the new custodian now called Signora Arnitz) arrived in Chesa Silvascina with the girls to spend the summer just a few days before the American Eighth Army landed among the prickly pears parched by the hot sun of Sicily. Vivia came over from Lugano to be with the inseparable Marisetta, and, as soon as he finished his university exams, Eddy boarded the train in Coira, and climbed up through the woods and valleys of Engadine, to join them.

The suitor with the slicked-back hair and pink lips made his reappearance on a hot July afternoon, pedaling energetically along the road that wound along the shoreline of the whitecapped lakes. His thesis, printed on glossy paper, was much admired by Signora Arnitz, who already envisioned him as an ambassador or statesman. And, sitting at the little table on the lawn, the young man had no difficulty demonstrating the accuracy of his past predictions, confidently spreading out on the tablecloth the newspapers he had brought with him from St. Moritz, packed tightly in the basket of his bicycle. Nobody dared contradict him anymore; and Signora Arnitz less than ever. And as she poured them tea in the ever-present sky-blue cups she already imagined him at Margot's side in an impeccable morning suit.

Shortly after his arrival, Eddy had a relapse of pleurisy and Margot took care of him, even to the point of getting up in the middle of the night to make him some hot milk and honey. In the silence of the darkened house she spoon-fed him like a baby to calm his cough, whispering and stifling her laughter to avoid waking Mamigna, just two doors away. A relapse that was surely caused by one of those nights out in the chalet, whooping it up and sweating, and then going out into the damp night air. That same summer, the suitor who had had such great success with his thesis on the early economic theories of Vilfredo Pareto asked Margot to marry him. There had even been a semiofficial visit from his parents, who came in especially from Zurich. Signora Arnitz pressed her to answer but Margot asked for time. Marriage, she said, hadn't brought good fortune to her family. She wanted to think about it, for at least six months.

But one night Marisetta found them kissing in the chalet. It was a very embarrassing scene, the aspiring bridegroom was visibly agitated, almost beside himself, and his lips, wet with saliva, kept searching for Margot's mouth. The fire was burning and Margot was lying on an old rug, her face colored by the flames. Marisetta closed the door in a rush, but when she got back to the house she couldn't resist announcing to Mamigna that the engagement was now final.

A misunderstanding, a stupid, unmitigated misunderstanding. Margot made a scene and Signora Arnitz had to swallow her joy over Marisetta's announcement. The next day Eddy had come down with a fever again.

But now the news from Italy is not at all reassuring and Signora Arnitz has decided to write to her daughter-in-law to convince her to let Marisetta stay through the winter. They'll all stay on at Chesa Silvascina, Vivia too, and Marisetta can continue her language courses at St. Moritz where even Margot has found an extraordinary voice teacher in the ex-Kapellmeister from Bratislava. The hotels are all crowded with refugees and there's no lack of teachers. As for Eddy, it's a whole different story, she says. Eddy is a full-fledged

Swiss citizen and he can decide to do whatever he likes. If he wants to stay on and keep the girls company, so much the better.

But perhaps Signora Arnitz isn't so enthusiastic about this second option. Eddy is better and standing in the living room looking out at the mountains that an unexpected summer snowfall has turned into immaculate peaks in the sky, a snow that seems to slide down and blend in with the wet, shiny meadows. He is the son of the man that to this day she identifies with "passion," a man that made her tremble with desire and writhe with jealousy. Years that memory has turned into a labyrinth she can't ever find her way out of; and on those solitary nights, in front of the colored pieces of the jigsaw puzzle, she retraces her steps back through it again and again, searching for the point that she went past without seeing. The missed place. She was as though crazed and blind in her race to find it.

Eddy is shaken again by a fit of coughing. His pants fall down around his thin body and an annoying cold forces him to keep blowing his nose. His face has become less round but no more virile, and he has none of the splendor that she had seen in the other. And yet some imperceptible sign, the way he moves his hands when describing something, the timbre, at times, of his voice. His mouth, oh yes, that angelically beautiful mouth. But how different in that big, pudgy face, marked by the circles of his glasses. A face that he surely got from his mother, that two-bit little slut. Eddy turns around, his glasses shining in that chilling light of a summer gone bad. He knows exactly what Signora Arnitz wants from him, as well as what she fears. His mother wasn't really the poor slut that she imagines. He has told her a lot of things, leaving others for her to intuit.

And surely Margot has understood too. But Margot avoids subjects that she says are "boring." Margot resists; and tenderness, when and if it breaks through, is a puff of air, a wispy, fleeting cloud. Her

sudden, fresh kisses. She has full, strong lips, like her body; eyes that
dart away and laugh. And then he can't keep up with her, follow her
in what has become her great passion. That damned *mysticism of the
mountains*. He can't thrill with her on the glaciers at the creaking of
the climbing irons, the pocketknife slicing through the apple in the
silence. The long hours of drinking in the shelters, dazed from the
altitude and fatigue, the warmth rising up inside like a fever. Afterward it's so wonderful to let yourself go, she says, to kiss and caress
each other until you feel your skin start to shiver.

The aspiring bridegroom with the pink lips can do that, yes, he
can, with that Luis Trenker body of his. But he has to go back to
Zurich now to prepare for a civil service exam to enter the diplomatic corps. An important family, Signora Arnitz says, Protestant
aristocracy. The young man's long, shapely fingers pass through his
hair to tidy it up, slick with brilliantine. He'll try to come for the
Christmas holidays and again for Easter and then Margot will
decide; they could get married at the beginning of next summer.
His words display confidence and he grabs Margot's chin with de-
termination to make her look him in the eye, the moist cigarette
dangling between his lips. Margot stares back at him, defiant, her
mouth opened slightly to show the shine of her teeth, a smile that
is playful and provocative at the same time. God, even ambiguity is
simple for this girl! The impulse to kiss her becomes irresistible and
he pulls her forcefully to him.

If only Eddy weren't always breathing down their necks. Every
time they turn around he's standing there behind them. And with
those crossed eyes of his you can never figure out where he's looking, what he wants (*how many times in the chalet, how many other
times in the mountain shelters, their throats warm with wine, or even
way up there on top, where the silence is broken only by the ravens?*).
Margot frees her chin from his hand with a jerk, the lips of the
young scion of the Protestant aristocracy press down nervously on
his cigarette, saliva bubbles in the corners of his mouth.

Margot probably would have said yes and then she would have become an attractive matron in Zurich with a lovely multistory house in Sonnenbergstrasse. She would have taken her dog out in the morning to the wood that climbs up the hillside, walking along leaf-covered paths and stopping to look down on the red roofs of the city. The wide, shining bend in the river. A sports lover, she would have won little trophies, cups made of silver and imitation gold, with the date inscribed on them and the name of her club. She would have gone to dinner at Königshalle and in the afternoon, together with some friends, she would have enjoyed a cup of tea at a table in the Dolder tearoom, letting her bored gaze lose itself in the dazzling expanse of the meadows.

Chesa Silvascina would never have been sold. Year after year, the snow carried in from the slopes would have melted on the ski rack in the vestibule, sliding down the edges of the skis, and the tennis court that was talked about every summer would finally have been built. Her former suitors would have come back to play singles with her, or mixed doubles, and the balls would have rolled along the circular drive before coming to a stop in the tall grass. Children would have jumped into the pool and shivered afterward in their robes that she would have rubbed energetically on their backs, and at sunset, before going back inside, their screaming and racing around would have scared off the little roe deer that had come down to graze at the edge of the woods. The chalet would have remained a special hideaway with its checkered curtains on the windows and the firewood piled in neat rows on the porch; and in all likelihood the Bentley would have been replaced by a fire engine red Ford with festive children in the windows.

Many years later when Lorenza went to visit her grandmother in the rest home in Geneva, Signora Arnitz was almost blind and sat all shriveled up in a wicker armchair on the veranda, the sharp red highlights of the sunset cutting into her face like a wound. But

Signora Arnitz was no longer able to notice; and with her arthritis-numbed fingers she tried to untie the package that Lorenza had placed on her lap. She showed no reaction at the name of Chesa Silvascina, almost as if it were not only a place unknown to her but which didn't interest her at all, and her lips, constantly in motion as if intent on eating themselves, remained silent. Lorenza helped her untie the gold thread and opened the box for her and she asked if they were Rossana candies. Rossana candies, she explained, were the only ones she liked. Only toward the end of the visit, when the light over Lake Geneva had dissolved into a uniform gray spotted with shadows, did she speak about the man to whom she attributed all her misfortune. *Ein Teufel*, a devil, she said.

From the moment she had set eyes on him she understood that he wasn't going to be just an ordinary guest. She had a lot of experience with people and she had seen right away that there was something different about him, something alarming. It's strange, she said, how your first impression always turns out to have been right. She always looked at people's hands; his were strong, dark, with hair on the back. He had introduced himself as a friend of Isabella's. What friend; probably he was her lover . . .

"You can't talk about Mamma like that," Lorenza interrupted her, "You can't." Even though she was now a scrawny, sickly old bird, wrapped up in her chair as in a nest dashed to the ground by the wind, her obtuse cruelty still cut Lorenza to the quick. "You can't. She was your daughter." She squeezed the box of candies on her lap. "Oh, children . . ." she said. Margot; surely she was thinking of Margot. Even though she would never have said her name.

Those hands were all scratched and one was wrapped in a handkerchief. He was dressed with a certain elegance, Zouave trousers and sturdy leather boots, but his heavy tweed jacket was smeared with mud and partly torn. "He took a bad fall right outside the gate," Margot said, "he could easily have broken his neck." But Signora

Arnitz was immediately suspicious because Margot introduced him as a friend of Isabella's. She never trusted Isabella's friends; Isabella always chose her friends in the wrong places. But then it came out that Doctor Zurhaus had sent him. Doctor Zurhaus had been their family doctor for years and she held him in great esteem. Later that evening the doctor called from Coira to see if Doctor Colin had arrived. That's exactly what he said, Doctor Colin. A brilliant scholar, he added, *eine hervorragende Persönlichkeit*.

Colin, French then? Signora Arnitz asked immediately. French, naturally, he answered, from Picardy. And she was instantly proud to talk about the battle of San Quentin, won by Emanuele Filiberto. But her guest had left his home town, Fourmies, as a child; and although he knew about the battle that had opened the way to Paris for the Spanish in 1557, he didn't know much about the region that was a prime bombing target every time there was a war.

The girls greeted the new arrival with enthusiasm. That winter there weren't the usual comings and goings at Chesa Silvascina and as soon as they heard that the new guest was French they took him upstairs to the room with the yellow chaise, singing a song by Josephine Baker. A really silly song; and then Signora Arnitz heard the water tumbling into the tub and the girls laughing and dancing around with the bath towels without much concern about who that man really might be.

Eddy lent him one of his jackets to go down to dinner. He had hardly any luggage and said he was expecting a trunk that was held up in some train station along the way. The temperature had dropped and there were so many stars it looked like the sky had been perforated with a hole punch, and the snow billowed up around the house, sparkling with ice crystals. After dinner the girls decided to take him out to the lake to let him admire the moon as it rose full round from behind Mt. Margna and stretched out its ghostly wings all the way to the Maloja pass. Even though he was exhausted, he followed them, covering his shoulders with a blanket

57

he had found in his room, and all together they walked along the snow-packed trail that skirted the current of the Inn. A stream that was to have such an important role in their relationship and that night it seemed to be flowing with milk as it glided along, so clear and fast through the snow-covered rocks, just a slight rustling sound along the banks, among the thorns white with snow.

But already at the dinner table (later on Signora Arnitz had had to admit it) her mistrust of the new guest had partially subsided. The light from the deer-antler lamp illuminated an uncommon and interesting face, and Doctor Colin showed an easy familiarity with the use of the various items of silverware. And even though he was obviously hungry he maintained through the entire meal an attitude of detachment toward what was on his plate, maneuvering gracefully through the conversation. He stated that he had a degree in medicine but that he was more of a researcher than a physician and that he was especially interested in algae. "In algae?" the girls exclaimed, "But in Switzerland we have no sea." "On the other hand there are lots of lakes," he rebutted, "and some very interesting ones too." Even in the lakes near their house, there were several species not to be found in other climates. But in response to the question of what he looked for in algae, he answered vaguely, talking about a long stay in Nice related to his work.

Signora Arnitz would have liked to know instead more about his friendship with Isabella, but that evening it seemed discourteous to insist. At the same time, listening to him talk, everything seemed simple and clear and his evident familiarity with foreign languages and cities made it easy to believe him. The girls listened to him, almost forgetting to eat in order to ask him continuous questions about France and Paris. About the German soldiers that occupied the hotels, snapped pictures from the top of Montmartre, and sat in the cafés along the boulevards. "Even the Folies Bergère, is it full of Germans there too?" Marisetta asked. "I don't know, but I imagine so, even the Folies Bergère," he smiled at the foolish ingenuousness of the question. It was the first time since he'd arrived; as if Marisetta's languid, enchanted eyes had freed his face from a cramp that kept it contracted. A quick smile, which was gone instantly. Nevertheless he had smiled. And Marisetta looked all around in triumph.

Those were good times in Chesa Silvascina. In the rest of Europe people were dying and suffering in the most frightening ways but up there the news was cushioned by all that snow, and the new guest seemed very careful from the very beginning to maintain the right distance between what he had left behind and what he had found at that table laid out with fine silverware and antique ceramic plates from Grisons. A table where the eyes, mouths, smooth and ruddy cheeks of the girls were a reminder that life was also beauty and levity. Amazement, joy. And this was probably just what Signora Arnitz wanted, that nothing disturb the calm in which she had found shelter after the turbulent years of her second marriage, years full of illusions and marked by blows inflicted without pity.

That past summer Eddy and the girls had already made friends among the circle of refugees from the war-torn countries, the rich refugees who wanted to continue skiing at Corviglia and Suvretta and drinking hot chocolate with whipped cream. Mountains of whipped cream and venison with blueberries. But this guest who had arrived as if he had just rolled down off of Mt. Margna certainly didn't have the air of independent wealth, and Signora Arnitz wanted to rest easy. The measures introduced by the authorities were clear, and she talked things over that same evening with Margot. She didn't want to end up like poor Gruniger, the police chief in San Gallo who had been convicted of aiding and abetting illegal refugees. But everybody knew what Margot was like. She couldn't care less about Mamigna's anxieties; she always thought everything was simple and easy while her mother was exaggerated or even melodramatic. And to calm her down she promised she would write to her aspiring bridegroom in Zurich. In Zurich he'd be able to obtain whatever information she wanted.

But Margot didn't write nor take it upon herself to ask him about anything; and she was never to see that would-be bridegroom again. Maybe she had already intuited the truth; maybe she knew. Isabella's letter had been rather confused, talking about *a favor, a big favor*, and she had always had that obtuse, foolish affection for her older sister. And though on that first night, together with Marisetta and Vivia, she had addressed the new guest with the formal "lei", the next day all three of them addressed him as "tu", and they had already invented a nickname for him, Franz, after the mysterious friend in the *Grand Meaulnes*. He seemed to be very happy with the room where they had set him up and he spent the mornings stretched out on the yellow chaise reading books that he selected from the bookshelf in the living room. The trunk had still not arrived and every day he went down to the post office to inquire about it, he said, and then he sat in his closed room and wrote long letters that he put in his pocket and that nobody ever saw.

After a week Signora Arnitz was already in a state of agitation. She wanted to know how much longer he'd be staying. There was no evidence that he had Swiss francs or any other currency, except for the small change he used to buy stamps, and in the evening he continued to use that heavy tweed jacket that Margot had asked Lula to patch. But he was very good at sitting next to Signora Arnitz and entertaining her with his observations about books or about the music that was broadcast on the radio. She sometimes surprised herself staring at him as he stood at the window looking down on the girls getting ready to go skiing in a din of cheerful voices. She saw him tall and erect, with his hands in his pockets and his hair, which grew down onto the back of his neck, dark and bristly. And she sensed his manly vigor, something that still aroused her and that she had never learned to resist. She liked the shape of his head, his shoulders, the way his hands in his pockets stretched the fabric of his pants over his narrow hips. Then he would turn and sit down next to her, pick up one of the pieces of the puzzle and instantly find the right place for it. But this too he always did with great attention, without intruding, and only when he understood that Signora Arnitz was in need of help.

From the very first day the girls had got it into their heads to teach him to ski, but apart from those brief trips to the post office, Doctor Colin seemed to prefer staying in the house and particularly up in his room with the yellow chaise. In the end he let himself be convinced, and he put on an old windbreaker that belonged to Alberto and followed them up through the valley that ran between Muott'Ota and Alp Munt. Uphill he was all right, he had stamina, but when he had to go downhill all he did was fall and Margot patiently went over beside him, helping him to get up when he sank into the snow, his poles pointing in opposite directions. And while the others went ahead, she waited for him and they joked about his clumsiness. But the second time he went with them, when the girls broke out laughing after his umpteenth fall, he rudely told Margot to stay away from him and tried to get back up on his own. Then he took off his skis and, up to his waist in snow, he started to rail at them and berate them. But his anger was directed mostly at Margot and he shouted at her that she was a foolish, spoiled girl. Flushed from fatigue, and covered with snow, he looked like a scarecrow with his hair straight up on his head. Margot tried to respond but he shut her up immediately, and he did the same with Eddy when he came over to help her. Suddenly he was a different person, and his strength was obvious. It wasn't so much physical strength, though it was that too, but above all it was strength of mind. Margot almost started to cry and she looked at him as he went off, his legs sinking deeper into the snow with every step as he refused to give up, falling and getting up again, pulled along by rage. His skis banging against his body.

It was Margot who found him again later on. That morning, after a brief moment in which she vented her anger, she became quiet until at a certain point she announced that she was going back to look for him. She left Eddy and the girls ready to start a new descent with the sun burning down and Mt. Margna sharp against the sky, the air so limpid you could make out the cascading traces left by little avalanches. One of those days they'd been anxiously awaiting for weeks, when the snow just opens up, turning to dust under your skis, and the shadows are tinged with azure. "What are you doing; forget about him," Eddy yelled back at her, "Nobody can stop that guy; he's got seven lives like a cat!" But Margot shook her head and Vivia and Marisetta saw her start down and then get smaller and smaller with the wind flapping her blue pants.

She found him in a shelter halfway back, one of those wood structures with smoke coming out of the chimney. She immediately recognized his skis, leaning against the rack outside the door, and suddenly her legs went limp, her fingers unable to set her poles down next to his, getting caught up in the wrist straps. It was that sense of happiness, an inner tremor and at the same time elation, that suddenly gave her the measure of how, in just those few days, that man was already inside her. He had occupied a space that she never would have thought herself capable of giving up to anyone.

"Don't call me Franz," he immediately attacked her, "I hate nicknames, and especially nicknames like that one." Because that was the first word that Margot had said when she saw him sitting at the table, a *Franz* that was a sigh of relief and joy. For her it was natural to call him that and to walk over to him. Now she had gone rigid again, her cheek bones standing out hard on her face gilded by the sun, her eyes still blinded by the reflection off the snow, closed tight behind her eyelashes. She felt like crying again. *Franz*, or whatever she was supposed to call him, looked at her: and suddenly made room for her next to him on the bench as if he had been waiting only to have her near him, and his hands pushed the old windbreaker out of the way, sinking down nervously into the material. For a moment Margot remained standing on the other side of the table, her sunglasses pulled up on top of her ski cap, her firm, girlish face with its small round chin red from the cold. She saw all of him, her memory was recording every detail but at the same time she felt as if she were blind to the reality of that face, it seemed to escape her and get lost among all that was around them (the smell of fried grease, the roughhewn boards of the tabletop, that empty glass that presumably had held only water). Then she let herself slide in next to him and their hands instantly intertwined in a tangle of fingers. His still bore the signs of his terrible fall from the Muretto pass. Margot could feel the hard, coarse scars under his fingertips as the tremor inside her slowly began to wane.

It was in that shelter, on that bench, that he spoke to her about his first failed attempt to cross over into Switzerland through the Alps of Upper Savoy in October '43. When he had been rejected at the border because *les réfugiés raciaux ne sont pas des réfugiés politiques*. And during the night, to avoid being handed over to the authorities at the French border, he had escaped to go back over the same harrowing route in the opposite direction. And he thought he was going to die. To die from exhaustion, to die at the bottom of a gorge or smashed against the rocks.

Margot had them bring her two bowls of barley soup, one for each, and she listened to him, softly caressing his fingers. Outside the window she could see the snow and the wood tips of the skis piercing the azure sky. "And then? Go on." She took her cap off and the ruffled hair on top of her head made her seem little more than a child. "Go on," she said again. But he sat there in silence: all of a sudden Mt. Buet, the Col de Vieux, and the Diosaz became *the place that was no place*, a pure invention compared to that soup with the little pieces of floating bacon, the spoon that went from

63

the bowl to that mouth moist with broth, barely opened as she listened, her eyes raised toward his, intense in the pink of her cheeks made brighter by the cold. "Then I went back to Italy," he said quickly, "The pastor of a small church in the French Alps helped me, got me all the equipment I needed to join up with a group of seminarians who were going back across the Alps to Piedmont." He took her face in his hands to move it closer to his: "All boys born and raised amid snow, while for me it was the first time I'd ever put on a pair of skis." Now their eyes were almost touching, "And you want me to enjoy myself with those two pieces of wood on my feet?" He pressed her against his chest and she felt the coarse wool of his sweater pricking her cheeks.

After that he never wanted to talk about himself again. Not even about that August of '42 when he stood outside the Hôtel Bompard in Marseilles as the French police loaded up the women and children who had been shut up in the hotel to deport them to Les Milles.

They made love in the chalet as the sky drew back from the small square of the window, cobalt blue around the first star, the snow that had stuck on the windowsill now leaden and gray. A violent love, consumed by its own desire, with no tenderness. Afterward Margot lay trembling from the cold and the wrenching of her body, Alberto's old windbreaker rolled up in a ball under her head. And when the voices of Marisetta and Vivia came through the crystal clear air and then died down into a confused murmur among the trees, she hurriedly got dressed and rushed to join them as they were going back into the house with their skis on their shoulders, the cold transforming itself into a long shiver almost as if she had a fever.

Signora Arnitz didn't suspect a thing. Everything continued as it had in the days before, with the girls going out on the balcony in the morning to see how the weather was so they could decide where to go, and then the usual argument with them and Eddy near the barometer, she protesting because Marisetta always found some excuse not to go to St. Moritz. Those language lessons were turning into a fairy tale. The guest went back to spending the day in his room behind closed doors and seemed for the moment to have given up on skiing. He read an entire shelf of books in just a dew days, mostly travel books that used to belong to Alberto, and spent the mornings at the table composing those mysterious letters that were supposed to procure him the money he needed to leave Chesa Silvascina and finally become part of the group of doctors of the Cimade.

"The 'Cimade'?" Signora Arnitz has never heard of it and as far as she's concerned he might as well use any other name or acronym. The Cimade, Margot explained to her later on, was an organization, a Protestant committee to aid refugees. Nothing mysterious about it. Just that as a physician, Doctor Colin seems out of practice and when asked for some medical advice he limits himself to recommending aspirin or cough drops, while demonstrating an incredible readiness to perform all kinds of mathematical calculations. An almost monstrous ability to resolve rebuses or to predict the innumerable solutions to a hypothesis. So much so that Signora Arnitz has gotten into the habit of consulting him when she has a problem with the bank or her accountant.

And if Vivia or Marisetta had understood anything or even been informed about what was happening, later on Signora Arnitz wouldn't be able to say. Margot's influence over them was such that they would never have been capable of betraying her or rebelling against her. From the start, the real obstacle was Eddy. Eddy's antennae were too finely tuned for him to be easily misled. And even if Margot always knew the best way to convince him, this time she would have to be more careful than before to keep from stirring up his resentment. But maybe Margot trusted a bit too much in that devotion, bordering on the idiotic, that Eddy displayed for her.

Signora Arnitz would never forget those noisy breakfast scenes when their voices, intermingled with laughter, found their way all the way up to her room. For years, *afterward*, she asked herself how it could have been that nothing in their behavior, their aggressive cheerfulness, had changed. That they could have been the same girls, the same Eddy, clumsy and kind, with those little glasses on his round, astonished face, talking and laughing in the light of the large windows, his fingers dripping with honey. Only he, only the *Teufel*, had not surprised her. And for years that image would continue to persecute her, together with the thought of how easy it had been to deceive her.

If only the slightest suspicion had ever flashed through her mind of what was happening right before her eyes. Never, never. If only she had perceived, even just for a moment, what might happen, and then actually did happen, just a few rooms away from her own. She, who boasted that she knew more about life than other people, looked at them with satisfaction as they sat around the breakfast table all talking at once, the bone handle knives spreading marmalade on slices of bread just out of the toaster; their mouths happily grinding up biscuits, walnuts, little dark loaves of rye bread as the sunlight, intensified by the snow, shines on the hand ready to pour the milk into the cup, sprays reflections off the pitcher; the aroma of the coffee mixing with the smell of the toast. The smell of a morning cold outside and warm inside. God, young people, she thinks, and goes into the kitchen ready to reprimand them for making too much noise, eating too much, waving their hands and arms around too much. Her eyes look around her and immediately notice the walnut shells on the carpet, the marmalade spilled on the white tablecloth. The cigarette crushed out in the bottom of a cup. They don't even notice her and continue talking in their incomprehensible lingo; then suddenly one of them laughs, her head tilted a little to the side and her lips oily with butter, her hand holding out a slice of bread with teeth marks in it. It's all so alive, so monstrously, overpoweringly alive, ready to enter eternity with their *caffellatte* and their honey, the ovaltine, the cocoa. And that *doctor*; as if he had forgotten the horror and the disgust, the eyes behind the window of the Renault scrutinizing the passersby to flush out the "Jew." His future a black hole.

It is a frightening winter. Every night tons of bombs are dropped on Germany and trains riddled with bullets are abandoned on the tracks, tumble over cliffs; but the sharp, strident voice of the Great Assassin keeps on hurling threats from loudspeakers across half of Europe. That phantasmagoric circus *Deutschland über alles* is falling apart among corpses rotting in the slime, floating on the rivers, and hanging from the gallows. Burning in the ovens. Everywhere, in Romania, in Bulgaria, in Croatia just as in Holland, in Belgium and France and in Moravia, in Italy or in Hungary, the *Sturmbann-führer*, whether they're named Bosshammer or Lerch or Tauss, carry out their systematic hunt for Jews. A game of precision that turns men into rat packs. Even in Switzerland, everywhere you look, all you can see are hooked crosses and barbed wire. In Parliament, the struggle to save at least the appearance of what had been their centuries-old liberality and tolerance has become bitter; and at night the refugees climb up into the mountains, slide down into ravines, drown in the rivers trying to find the safety that no one is prepared to offer them. Others fall under the rifle shots of the guards positioned behind chevaux-de-frise, as happened on the border at Saint-Julien. Still others, to avoid being taken back, kill themselves. "They poisoned themselves with a bottle of pills they were carrying," Marisetta says, "I read it in the *Tribune de Genève.* "Yes, that's right; I read it too," Vivia says, "Two Jews, I don't know if they were Polish or what, it happened at the border crossing in Forsanette."

A leaden horizon that reminds Signora Arnitz of a film she's seen recently, *Lost Horizon*, a film about the land of eternal youth.

But as soon as anyone crosses the border, old age kills them instantly, like some evil gas.

The chalet was an ideal meeting place. It was isolated and protected by the trees, outfitted with a strong lock. And even though it wasn't possible to light a fire in the fireplace because it could be seen from the windows, there were always some covers lying around, and every chance she could, Margot brought along her fur blanket.

It had always been a privileged place ever since she was a little girl and Mamigna was chasing after all of her "fiancés." A place well-suited for secrets and encounters, amorous and otherwise; but looking back on them, Margot's amorous encounters before that winter had been very innocent, limited to a few kisses and some petting. Even with Eddy; more of a game than anything else, a cautious and timid exploration eased by lots of tenderness. Margot was jealous of her body and even with the young man who seemed destined to become her husband, the aspiring bridegroom from Zurich, she was always careful to stop him in time. To free herself at the right moment from what she considered to be an intrusion on her *intangibilis hortus*. Maybe it was a reaction against her mother, against those scenes she had observed as a child, of dresses hurriedly put back in place and lies lined up one after another. All of those "fiancés" with whom Mamigna behaved so allusively like a girl with her first crush, or struck poses like a femme fatale. Chased after and pushed away behind trees and slamming doors; but whom she had certainly not forbidden from incursions into her private *hortus*.

A thought that was still very present in the mind of Signora Arnitz. And even though time and the vicissitudes she had been exposed to over the years had cooled her impulses, they had compensated for that by leaving her with that obsession in her head. An old feminine intuition that could not but recognize in the unusual guest so warmly recommended by Doctor Zurhaus an antagonist of a remarkably high caliber. She likes to look at him when he enters the living room to get a book or put it back on the shelf, likes listening to his voice and having him seated on the other side of the table where the puzzle is spread out, following the movements of his rough, nervous hands as they find the place for a piece that she had been looking for in vain. Strong fingers with flat fingertips, surely sensitive to touch, the cigarette barely pressed between his index and middle fingers and his face furrowed by two vertical wrinkles, extremely attractive. Something that only she, with her experience, is able to appreciate. Not those young girls ready to go into ecstasy over photographs of Robert Taylor or Errol Flynn. How else would it be possible to explain how she, so anxious about that Zurich marriage that she became furious when Margot and Eddy closed themselves up in the chalet, wasn't worried now about the presence in the house of such an uncommon man. *Racé* in the masculine sense, *ein echter Mann*, as she would have said at one time, as if she thought he could be appreciated only by palates of refined taste. Not by mouths that have only begun to chew, incapable of distinguishing between flavors.

And isn't Margot all sport and *camaraderie*? Ever since she started taking voice lessons in St. Moritz she seems to have nothing else in her head and the ex-Kapellmeister, she says every time she comes home, is very happy with her. At the dinner table she often talks about music with Doctor Colin; but while Margot becomes instantly enthusiastic he maintains an air of bland detachment. Surely an *hommes à femmes* but one who knows the rules of hospitality.

If Signora Arnitz had never been able to understand the value of tenderness, how important it was for Margot, and how much Eddy had adapted by now to the impossibility of a true gesture of love on her part, Margot too has underestimated those almost fraternal kisses, the long talks lying on the pillows in front of the fireplace in the chalet. Those light caresses, cautious and instantly disavowed, that so alarmed her mother. Now that a new feeling has arrived on the scene she no longer has either the time or the desire for those games. A *feeling* (Margot wouldn't know what else to call it) that sharpens all perception and that she is unable to deal with on a rational level. For the first time the relationship is frontal, she has a man opposite her with whom she wants to share everything. Food, time, sleep. The love they make in the chalet isn't enough for her; afterward she wants to go back up the stairs in the darkness embracing him, slide into his bed and snuggle up against his body, sleep wrapped around each other. She doesn't want to defend herself anymore or keep anything secret. Even though she knows that at the slightest hint of what's going on her mother is ready to set off a war in which pity would be the great missing element.

But Signora Arnitz is unperturbed; so much so that she decides to leave with the Bentley and the custodian behind the wheel dressed as a chauffeur. A diplomat friend of hers has managed to get her some gasoline coupons and she's going to Lausanne and Geneva where she is greatly revered in the banks. The evening before she'd also heard the good news that Doctor Colin has finally received the long-expected letter and in a few days he'll be leaving for his final destination. And that morning when the custodian from Unterwalden, buttoned up to his neck in his blue uniform, packed the two dark, stiff suitcases into the car, Signora Arnitz and the guest bid each other a very cordial farewell. He has thanked her with that smile of his, barely visible, the narrow, bony face still impenetrable. She thinks it's a final good-bye and gives her best performance, plunged into her fur coat, her foot already up on the running board. It has snowed during the night and there's a soft layer of new snow on the icy surface of the pool, on the fields and the road, and the guest bows in deference with his ice cold nose almost touching her hand. Margot says good-bye to her from the doorway; she's ready to go skiing and her red sweater embroidered with two deer heads sticks out from under her windbreaker. It starts snowing again and white flakes whirl about before coming to rest on the shiny hood of the car.

Eddy arrived when the custodian in his new role was starting up the engine. He's always last and he sticks his panting face right inside the car, his sweet, beautiful mouth that seems to smell of milk. He wishes her a good trip and tells her to come back soon, as soon as she can, and places his hand over hers on the lowered window glass. At that point Signora Arnitz was overcome by a bolt of affection and gave him a quick caress on the cheek: Eddy must know that although she's opposed to a romance between him and Margot, that doesn't mean she loves him any less. On the contrary, she loves him even more. Then the car slipped away with the custodian steering cautiously, careful not to skid in the fresh snow, and Eddy bent over to pick up his glasses, which in the last-minute effusion had ended up on the ground. It was then that his gaze fell on the two of them still standing in the doorway, waiting to watch the Bentley's rear window disappear into the distance, the feather on Mamigna's green hat waving back and forth. And as he straightens up and puts his glasses back on, his eyes focus on the deer on Margot's sweater, her hair escaping out from under her beret. Doctor Colin's heavy tweed jacket and his hands in the pockets with just the thumbs sticking out, red from the cold. He kept staring at them for a minute as if he were hypnotized: the "uncontainable desire" rippling outward from the pallor of their faces like water hit by a stone. They don't seem to notice anything but suddenly Margot's eyes meet his. It's an instant; Eddy immediately turns red, she glares at him in anger. Then she turns brusquely and goes into the house. Doctor Colin is left standing in the door alone with his hands in his pockets.

That was to be the last morning they would go skiing together. Before noon, with the excuse that she was cold, Margot went back home. Eddy offered to go with her, the visibility was poor and she might lose her way. Without even stopping to listen to him, in just a few seconds she was a dark silhouette fading away into the snow, her red beret standing out against all that gray. For the rest of the day Eddy and the girls kept on skiing listlessly, but none of them had the courage to say what he was thinking. And when they got back to Chesa Silvascina in the afternoon the house was silent and dark; all they could hear was the gramophone playing in the room with the yellow chaise. But nobody dared knock on Doctor Colin's door to ask if he knew where Margot was.

She didn't show up until dinner time, brash and self-assured as always, and her exaltation was almost palpable, it seemed as if she could feel it on her skin, breathe it in through her mouth, swollen and tired looking. Her small warm hands kept reaching for the cool of the silverware as her blue wool dress, which she had always despised as too feminine, now accentuated the full curves of her breasts. A challenge? Or was it just the first that she happened to pick up, the one that's easy to slip into like a pullover? Her big eyes, slightly bewildered, are looking out at the snow that has started coming down again. "They'll have closed the Majola pass and the Julier too," she says, "Mamigna must have made it through just in time . . ." and then suddenly, under the gaze of Vivia and Marisetta, she turned red for the too obvious satisfaction expressed in those words.

But afterward she was just hungry and not much inclined to conversation. She was particularly aggressive with Eddy, making fun of him because he tripped over his words, something that happened to him when he was upset. Almost to the point of cruelty when she reproached him for always carrying a picture of her. "It's a terrible picture, and besides it's at least three years old," she said, "The least you could do is choose a better one, all you ever do is take pictures." "I like that one," he answered without looking at her, "It was your best moment; since then you've only gotten

72

worse." His cross-eyed squint accentuated by the tension like a hub pushed off its axle; a total fiasco.

Doctor Colin didn't come down to dinner. In the few days that he was to remain at Chesa Silvascina, Vivia and Marisetta would see him only rarely; most of the time Margot would prepare him a dinner tray and take it up to his room. Almost a provocation in the creaking of the wood as she went up the stairs with the tray in her hands. Not in too much of a hurry, but not too slow either, so the soup or the omelet wouldn't get cold.

5

The telegram from Marisetta asking her to come home immediately reached Signora Arnitz in Geneva. But the passes were still
closed and the telephone lines were buried under mountains of
snow. The operators tried in vain to make the phone ring under the
big portrait of Alberto as the snow kept falling and falling, weighing down the limbs of the larch trees to the breaking point. And
each passing minute erased lost gloves and crumpled photographs,
footprints overlapping as they sank deeper into the snow among
the frozen bushes on the banks of the Inn.

When the sun finally came out again and the Bentley managed
to climb back up the circular drive through the unbroken white-
ness of the snow, Signora Arnitz found Chesa Silvascina wrapped
in an unreal silence and Vivia and Marisetta closed in their room,
puffy circles under their eyes and that beautiful color they'd got
from skiing washed away, turned ashen by the tension. *Margot's
gone.* Yes, Mamigna must know about it right away. Margot has
gone away with that man she had so incautiously let stay at their
house for weeks. A Jew, Eddy had discovered him.

A Jew? And how did Eddy figure it out? But Eddy's not there,
Vivia and Marisetta don't know where he's gone and they shrug
their shoulders to avoid the wrath of Signora Arnitz. They contradict each other. So at first she gets the idea that Eddy has followed
the other two, impulsive as he is; and Vivia and Marisetta are too
scared to correct her. Even though it's an absurd hypothesis; the
drawers in his room are full of clothes, his skis are still there in the
vestibule leaning up against the wall, his beret and goggles wound

up in the wrist straps of the poles. All he took was his fur jacket and he didn't tell anyone where he was going.

Not even you two? No, all he said was something about the postal coach, maybe yes, at a certain point he said something about going to catch the coach. The coach, to go where? I don't know, he didn't tell us, all he said was the coach, I swear, Lula heard it too.

Nobody tells Signora Arnitz about the horrible fight in the room with the yellow chaise. How at a certain point Marisetta went into the room frightened by Margot's screaming and saw Doctor Colin holding onto Eddy by his sweater and looking like he was just about to throw him against the wall, Margot screaming and trying to stop him. As she entered the room she stepped on a pair of glasses and there was a towel on the chaise covered with blood; she wasn't sure if it was Eddy's or Margot's. Then Doctor Colin let go and she saw Eddy with his lip split open, his eyelids batting over his wide eyes, unable to see straight. But he didn't seem at all frightened; and as soon as he could move freely he pushed Margot away as she tried again to wipe the blood off his chin. He was white. Marisetta had never seen Eddy like that; he was trembling with rage and kicked his glasses away, sending them tumbling down the stairs.

But nobody has the courage to tell all this to Signora Arnitz and Signora Arnitz has other things to think about than Eddy's absence. As if she weren't used to his strange behavior, a boy capable of getting on a train to Zurich for nothing more than a dinner invitation. Was she supposed to worry about him now too? Oh no, not on your life!

The blow inflicted by Margot, that, yes, is terrible. Terrible and cruel. She can't bring herself to accept it and she is willing to use any means to bring her back to reason. But she has to find out where she's gone; and she yells at Vivia and Marisetta because she's convinced they're hiding something from her. She doesn't realize that the more she yells the more they retreat behind their mumbled half-sentences that don't say anything.

76

But Switzerland isn't France; it's not so easy to disappear and cover your tracks. . . . She rummages around in the room with the yellow chaise, but *that one* came with nothing and he had gone with nothing. The drawers are empty; all that's left in the wardrobe are a pair of Margot's slippers (now all the thoughts that come into her head are intolerable. She doesn't even want to touch those slippers. Lula, who is helping her with the inspection, has a malicious grin on her face that she pretends not to see).

So then everyone knew and nobody said anything, nobody had thought to warn her. But now there is no one who doesn't protest his innocence. All she finds is surprise and dismay. Margot's room is still all topsy-turvy as if she had been in a tremendous hurry to leave. She goes through the music books on the table; she could at least have left a note, two lines to ask forgiveness for stabbing her in the back like that. She feels like the Virgin transfixed by the Seven Sorrows, and at each new piece of evidence of what had been going on in those rooms, just a few steps from her own, a new thorn pierces her flesh. And when the aspiring bridegroom calls from Zurich she stammers out some nonsense to leave an opening for that idyllic future of respectability and wealth. The young man talks about his success on the civil service exam. He finished in the top three, he tells her. Signora Arnitz tries to put some cheer in her voice: Margot, yes, she'll be coming home shortly; she's gone on an outing. He knows how Margot is; with all that snow she just couldn't resist. . . .

Her first thought was to try to find Doctor Zurhaus. It was he who had recommended that damned guest. But Doctor Zurhaus had changed his address, and when Signora was finally able to track him down after a lot of failed attempts, he sounded as if he'd been struck by lightning. He had met Doctor Colin in Paris before the war, he said, a fine young man and a great scholar. People like him deserve to be helped. And his voice, a little coarse with age, expressed more reproach for Signora Arnitz's lack of solidarity than

77

contempt for the behavior of her guest. He even cited a saying in Latin, *mala tempora currunt* but it seemed he was referring more to the measures taken by the Swiss authorities with regard to refugees than to what she had called to complain about. Signora Arnitz hated him.

Vivia wants to go back to her parents in Lugano and Marisetta asks to go with her. She implores her to let her go; but Signora Arnitz will not hear of it; she's got enough *cauchemars* already, she says, she doesn't need any more worries from Marisetta. By now she doesn't trust anyone; and after an initial impulse to call the police, she's now afraid of a scandal. Of an investigation. The laws are clear; she should have reported her guest to the police immediately. There's even a provision of the Military Code. She had gone cautiously to ask for information and they told her that "facilitating the illegal entrance or exit into or from Switzerland, or providing your own assistance to that end, is punished in the worst cases with detention." They showed her the text of the law: *Whoever shall give asylum to refugees without authorization of the competent Police Authorities shall be punished in accordance with Article 107 of the Military Criminal Code.* And a Jew to boot; ignorance of the law is no excuse.

Marisetta closed herself off into a hostile silence. Then she changed tactics, going around the house with a pained look on her face, melancholy and depressed. But Mamigna does not allow herself to be moved: you've got a lot of other friends, she says, all you have to do is get on the coach or make a phone call. It's a beautiful sunny day and the snow couldn't be better. You girls are never satisfied.

She's written a fiery letter to Isabella; Isabella is responsible for the whole thing. But who knows when, or if, that letter will arrive. The Anglo-Americans have landed in Anzio and Field Marshal Kesselring has other things on his mind than making sure Signora Arnitz's letter arrives at its destination. The few trains that still manage to make it over the border are subjected to continuous machine-gun fire and Mussolini's great adventure "by air, by land and by sea" has now been transformed into a rag-tag army in retreat.

Then one morning Margot called. She's in a railway station. She doesn't say where, but she is happy and well. She wants everyone's news; she asks about Eddy: how is he, is he still there? "Eddy? And who's seen him since?!" But Signora Arnitz suddenly realizes that she doesn't want to talk to her anymore. Her pain has given way to offense, sullen, irreparable, and she remains silent while on the other end of the line Margot's voice is shrill, don't worry about me she says, I'm fine, I'm happy. "But he's a Jew," she answers with a knot in her throat. "I know, I've always known, so what? I want to help him." Mamigna can't manage to say a word, feeling so sorry for herself she's about to be overwhelmed. She who almost never loses control is afraid she'll start crying on the telephone. Ah, that voice of Margot's that starts to fill with pity in response to her silence and tells her to stay calm: the war will be over soon she adds, and everything will be the way it used to be. She's happy, she says again. She loves him; he's such a wonderful man. "I wish he were dead," Signora Arnitz murmurs, "dead." And then all she heard was a buzz. Margot had hung up.

After that telephone call Signora Arnitz's worries turned in another direction. Should she get in touch with Eddy's mother or not, "that two-bit little slut" whom she'd never wanted to have anything to do with? But her doubts were resolved some days later by the "slut" herself, who called all upset because she hadn't heard from her son. Eddy normally wrote to her at least once a week, maybe just a post card, and now it had been three weeks without as much as a line or a phone call. But Signora Arnitz couldn't ease her worries. She couldn't explain his silence either, she said. Besides he'd left his drawers full of clothes and even his pajamas hanging in the bathroom. It was a long conversation and at a certain point it sounded as though Signora Arnitz was almost blaming the mother

79

for her son's lack of regard for her. As for Margot's running away and the ungrateful guest who had repaid her generosity so crassly, she didn't say a word.

They talked on the phone again over the next few days and in the end Signora Arnitz let her know that she was irritated by all this insistence. But by now her peace was lost, more like the pile of ashes in the fireplace that she sat contemplating every evening, having lost all desire to spread out on the table the new jigsaw puzzle she'd brought back from Geneva. The atmosphere in the house had become leaden and the cook who had been with her for many years and had held Margot in her arms as a baby wasn't able to hold back her tears as she stood over the burners, while Lula seemed possessed by an extraordinary zeal for continuously finding new evidence to confirm the affair between Margot and Doctor Colin.

Marisetta let herself be seen only rarely. As soon as she came back in from skiing she closed herself in her room only to reappear at dinner time with her eyes heavy with sleep, not in the mood for entertaining Mamigna; and that famous language course that she was supposed to have followed in St. Moritz wasn't talked about anymore. So a few weeks before Easter Signora Arnitz had found nothing better than to move with her niece to Lugano in one of the hotels on the lakeshore that hadn't been requisitioned. As good a way as any to rid herself for an indefinite period of the cook and the chambermaid, two rather inconvenient witnesses whom she sent home for a long and, she hoped, healthy vacation. This way Marisetta could be together with her inseparable friend and she could have some peace looking out on the placid mirror of the lake where the mountains were reflected foggily in the beating rain.

Because all it did was rain and the people scurried around bumping into each other with the points of their umbrellas. Signora Arnitz watched them from the big windows in the dining room as waiters crowded around their table, where Marisetta had turned talkative again. The rationing didn't affect them except with regard to certain foods and fish which used to be brought in from the Baltic and the maître d' pirouetted around them with the menu cursing the war that had driven away the rich English tourists, leaving behind only a bunch of poor refugees. Marisetta ate with a good appetite and the pianist in the corner looked at her as he played *Smoke Gets in Your Eyes*. Or, if he was in a good mood, *Lambeth Walk*.

At Chesa Silvascina the custodian emptied the water pipes so they wouldn't burst in an end-of-season freeze and battened down the shutters. His wife folded up the blankets inside the closets, sprinkling them with moth balls; and when two policemen, contacted by the military police in Lucerne, came by to ask a few questions of the owner, all the custodian could do was give them the address of Signora Arnitz in Lugano and show them the two suitcases already packed with well-folded clothes, the Kodak put back in its case, in the event the boy reported missing by his mother should return to reclaim his things. Other than that he didn't know a thing and had never noticed anything strange or different. *Gar nichts, nie!* He held out his arms like a priest blessing the faithful, as a guarantee that everything, always, had proceeded in the most normal fashion. Good-looking kids, friendly and polite, even if a bit noisy at times. *Jugend macht lustig*; he didn't like the house being empty.

Later he called Signora Arnitz to tell her about the visit and in his loud, rumbling voice he repeated for her one by one the words he had said to the police to reassure her that everything had gone as she had wished. Before leaving, in fact, the "*gnädige Frau*" had admonished him not to talk to anyone about the unpleasant affair of the guest who had stayed with them in the room with the yellow chaise. A regrettable incident that can happen to people of a certain class, accustomed to receiving friends from all over the world. *Mit niemandem, nie*. And she had compensated him in advance for the discretion she said she was sure she could count on.

And when the Lugano police called Signora Arnitz in for a face-to-face meeting with the mother of the missing boy, she had to admit that with time the "slut" had learned to talk and dress, and the meeting was quite civil. But in the end she was forced to confess the falling out with her younger daughter and that she didn't know where Margot was at the moment. She reiterated her impression that Eddy had followed her, a hypothesis she argued for fairly strongly not least because everybody knew, she said, how attached Eddy was to Margot.

As for the rest of it, Signora Arnitz felt she had every right to lie. She had been much too generous, even with Eddy, and it seemed unfair to her now to be dragged into a situation of which she had been the first victim.

Without remorse but not without a certain agitation, she headed back toward the hotel that rose up tall and glittering in the twilight, the ever-present flag with the white cross waving on its standard against the blue sky, where long patches of calm were opening up among the livid gray clouds. Marisetta was waiting for her among the semideserted armchairs of the lounge, holding a Persian cat on her lap while the pianist played *Tea for Two*, his melancholy gaze lost in the sparkle of the lake. "Finally," she said, getting up to meet her, the cat gliding down with a soft bounce onto the carpet, "I was beginning to think they'd arrested you!" Without taking his hands off the keyboard the pianist turned to look at her, smiling: that girl was a constant surprise. But Signora Arnitz didn't appreciate the joke.

That threat she had imagined she could avoid by closing up Chesa Silvascina and sending Lula and the cook on vacation was now represented in flesh and blood in the form of that former cosmetics counter salesgirl who had given birth to Eddy. And at night, turning over and over again between the sheets every time some muffled steps on the carpet in the corridor came to a sudden stop in front of a door, Signora Arnitz was shaken by a chill almost as if she had heard the screeching of a blade sawing through the floor around her. Among all her fears one in particular scared her the most: that something irreparable might happen to Margot.

At times she couldn't resist and slipped into Marisetta's room in her dressing gown. She wanted to know; get her to tell her what she suspected her niece was still hiding from her. But Marisetta was sleepy and looked up with her dilated pupils at that round body, wrapped up like a mushroom in the velvet robe, she didn't know and couldn't bring herself to imagine anything, not where Eddy had ended up nor where Margot might be. *Or the other one either, the Jew*; and she complained that she wanted to sleep. Then Signora Arnitz's ramblings became even more intense, enumerating the various hypotheses that might loosen the grip of her anxiety, the pauses between one sentence and the next marked lugubriously by the rare passage of a car on the shoreline drive, thumping over a loose manhole cover. Marisetta yawned and just wanted to forget. Forget the blood-soaked towel and the screaming, Eddy's contorted face, the threats yelled as he gave that senseless kick to his glasses and bolted down the stairs.

With the onset of the spring thaw Chesa Silvascina and the town were hit by a tempest of wind and rain that transformed the Inn, barely visible and silent under the cushions of snow, into a raging stream of tree trunks, tossed about and broken, whole bushes disappearing under the swirling current. The strips of ice still hanging on in the center of the lake began to split with a dull roar, a background groan that went on all through the night under the foliage snapping and crashing in the wind.

The custodian who had gone out to make sure the gusts hadn't ripped the doors off their hinges was left trapped inside the house. The electricity went out and in a second the road had turned into a torrent, dragging rocks and tree branches as the wind pulled off some of the shutters, shattering the window glass. Then with what sounded like a bomb blast one of the chimneys caved in, sliding down off the roof to crash against the slabs of stone around the edge of the pool.

Never seen anything like it, the custodian told the "*gnädige Frau*," as soon as the telephone lines had been restored, *als ob das ganze Haus in den Händen des Teufels wäre*, he screamed into the receiver. But fortunately, Chesa Silvascina, though with its flower beds invaded by glass, continued to offer the new spring sun its beautiful façade of stone and wood, offended only by the empty orbits of the windows.

Eddy's body was found a week later, stuck in the narrow passage between Lake Silvaplana and the smaller Lake Champfèr. For a long time it had been protected by the snow but in the final surge the force of the water had ripped away almost all the clothing. Some garments couldn't be found but others, like his socks and fur jacket, were upstream, not far from the intersection of the road and the stream; and inside the pockets, soaked with water and reduced to mush, some photographs had been found, unrecognizable.

For Signora Arnitz the inquest that followed was a torment. Consternation and horror gave way to fear accompanied by an irremediable certainty of guilt. For days and days she repeated obstinately her version of the tragedy. It couldn't have been anything other than an unfortunate accident, she insisted. And although there was nothing that appeared to contradict her, there wasn't much to support the hypothesis of an accident either. Eddy drank as much as young people normally drink and that afternoon when he left never to come back again, even though the snow had intensified at twilight, it was still the hour they called "between the dog and the wolf," when it's still possible to make out details on the road, the sparkle of the frozen spring and the outline of the bridge between the two light poles. To end up in the water he would have had to force his way down to the banks of the Inn; why should he ever have done that? He slipped, she insisted, it was very cold and the road must have been a sheet of ice. But there's a big difference between slipping on the roadway and ending up in the water. He could have been seized by a sudden urge, and gone down there on purpose. . . . But if he had drowned, sooner or later he would have had to surface somewhere or other; and from what little it was possible to understand, there were no visible signs of death by drowning. In all likelihood he had died from a cardiovascular collapse, as if he had suffocated. Suffocated? He must have had a syncope, poor boy! My God, everyone knew he had respiratory problems, his pleurisy was an old story!

Signora Arnitz was a woman accustomed to giving orders and now she was lending her authority to a version that left a lot of things in the dark. From the very first time she had been ready to deny involvement in that disappearance: never a conflict between herself and Eddy, or between Eddy and the girls. A version that was also confirmed at the time by Vivia and Marisetta. And now that there was the possibility of an inquest, the two girls repeated the same things they had said back then; Marisetta especially was very convincing in describing the atmosphere of *camaraderie* that reigned at Chesa Silvascina.

But in the end, to balance the accounts, Signora Arnitz was forced to open the purse strings several times and pull out thousands and thousands of francs to line Lula's pockets. And no one could say when it would be over. Luckily, the cook had always favored Margot; she would never betray her. With her all she'd had to do was ask; and now Signora Arnitz had scruples about whether she should give her a present.

She finally decided on a *renard argenté*, one of those foxes with four long-nailed paws and the round glass eyes that hung on the mannequins in the windows on Via Besso. The cook started to cry. She almost didn't want it; but Lula kept on making her requests: once because her nephew was sick and needed medical care, another time because there was a tobacco shop for sale that would solve all her problems. And sitting in a bar in Mendrisio Signora Arnitz looked at the face of her former chambermaid, pulled back by the heavy black braids wound into a crown on her head, her skin an oily pallor with no wrinkles. A face that might be ideal for someone who had to serve at table with an apron and white gloves, but that on top of that longhaired olive green overcoat looked gross and odious to Signora Arnitz. Or maybe it was the blackmail that forced Lula into that grimace of feigned submission, as her hand, almost as if it weren't hers, let the envelope with the money slide into her purse without even glancing at it, so as to demonstrate the trust she had in the word of "*gnädige Frau*" as she and the cook called her, imitating the custodian from Unterwalden. And Signora Arnitz looked away from that pallid face and the olive overcoat as though she had to wash them from her conscience as she asked herself how many more times she would have to sit opposite her at that bar crowded with working people, where you couldn't breathe from the smoke and the smell of bad wine.

Ever since Marisetta had decided to tell her about the terrible fight in the room with the yellow chaise, Signora Arnitz understood that that was the weak point. The crack that could open up into a hole so big that everything would come crashing down. She, the "slut," wanted nothing more than to trap her. And that was exactly why she wanted no one to have the slightest suspicion about what had happened on that afternoon. And although Signora Arnitz was smart enough to realize how important that was, Lula was too. All the more so since *Doctor Colin* was becoming much more than a shadow and his presence, like a spirit evoked by a medium, was steadily taking on more of a form and a voice. Even the manager of a shelter, up in the mountains, on the ski slopes, remembered having seen him sitting at a table with Margot.

If only Margot had contacted her. Had clarified for her what had really happened. They could have talked it over together, come up with an explanation that would shut Lula up and put a stop to her endless requests for money. But after that one telephone call Margot hadn't even sent a postcard. Not even to Vivia or Marisetta, as if she'd decided not to trust anyone. Now that the good weather had arrived her lovely spring suits were still hanging in the wardrobes at Chesa Silvascina, together with her shoes all lined up in a row under a thin layer of dust; and Signora Arnitz couldn't imagine how she was able to manage without any money, with what few necessities she had been able to take with her in the rush to get away that night. She was even afraid to ask about her, to inquire whether she had been in contact with anyone they knew. But above all she was afraid that if Eddy's death wasn't resolved in a hurry the police would make it their business to track her down.

At the beginning of the summer, thanks to the discreet intervention of some friends, the inquest was closed and Eddy's death recorded as an accident. His mother had come to get his two suitcases, cursing Chesa Silvascina; and when she saw his skis with his beret and goggles wound around one of the poles, she broke down crying. Vivia was very nice and had come, together with Marisetta, to greet her, carrying an envelope with the last photographs taken on Mt. Suvretta. The mother wanted her to have the Kodak, insisted that she take it, and then she collapsed on her shoulder. But she seemed to have developed an instinctive antipathy for Marisetta, and when the girl came over to embrace her she turned her head away.

Right after that, Marisetta announced she wanted to go to a pension in Neuchâtel and Signora Arnitz didn't object. By now she felt a kind of mental paralysis. She was no longer able to decide and command following her impulses, and her relationship with her granddaughter had become cautious, almost suspicious. All their conversations slid into falsely grave tones, while the truth, which by now was becoming clearly outlined in both their minds, remained the great outsider.

87

Later on, as springtime came into its own, the hotel took on a more cheerful air. The flowerpots returned, overflowing with colors, and the pianist renewed his repertoire. Signora Arnitz spent hours on the terrace looking over the lake, conceding a formal smile when some old acquaintance came over to chat. In the evening, among the clatter of plates and voices, she looked out through the open windows in the dining room, watching the motor boats with all their lights on cutting through the black water of the night. She followed its flow from one shore to the other, the notes of the piano providing the cadence for its gentle fluctuation. After Marisetta left, the maître d' preferred to concentrate his rotation around other tables and the pianist too stopped turning to look her way, his head with the hair glued to his skull bent over the keyboard to follow the tireless movement of his hands.

The streets were full of life and the variety of their sample of humanity served Signora Arnitz as a distraction. After the Anglo-American landing in Normandy, the authorities had "loosened the strings a bit too much," as she liked to say; and Lugano, almost as if a box had been opened, filled from one day to the next with all kinds of refugees. They were everywhere, in the cafés and at the cinema. In the cultural associations, where they gave lectures. A law passed on 12 July 1944 granted Jews the status of "*foreigners seriously threatened in their lives and integrity*" and Signora Arnitz wondered where Margot was now—together with that man that she had looked at with such satisfaction when his figure took on its full form, tall and erect, his hands stretching the fabric of his pants, as he stood in front of the window at Chesa Silvascina. Maybe now Margot would get in touch with her, perhaps just to ask for money; and every time she came back into the hotel Signora Arnitz glanced up at the pigeonhole with her room key hoping to find a message.

She didn't want to go back to Chesa Silvascina. The thought of being back in those rooms all alone except for the cat was gray, devoid of pleasure. The winding, rocky road that climbed up through the darkness of the woods of Upper Engadine now appeared to her to be an arduous, exhausting journey, infinitely melancholy. And so she thought of selling. But it wouldn't be easy; and for many years the photograph of Chesa Silvascina with the swimming pool and its wooden balconies, the *Alpenrosen* and the *Eisenhüte*, the red currant bushes, would stay pinned to the bulletin board of the real estate agency, while the custodian in his leather apron kept on mowing the lawn in the vain expectation of a visit from the "*gnädige Frau.*"

Once the summer heat had passed, she intended to move to Geneva. She had lived there for several years after her second marriage and Margot was born there. She didn't feel too old to change her life and she hoped that some of her friends who had been faithful over time would console her for the ingratitude of her children. In the morning, if it wasn't too hot, she would get on a bus and ride through the towns that looked out over the green water of the lake. The houses had flowers on the windowsills and more flowers overflowed from the gardens surrounded by hedges. Girls in bathing suits lay in the sun on the wooden docks, the small, invisible waves lapping softly among the pilings. Other girls. Carefree and cheerful. Other bathing suits. With vivid colors.

6

There she is! Margot! Lorenza and Marta waved their arms wildly from the balcony to greet her. Margot was crossing the street between the jeeps and the bicyclists, the white collar of her blouse folded over the lapel of her jacket, her face smiling in the sun. Arturo was walking beside her as they'd always seen him. Nothing was changed and even his jacket seemed the same, hanging loosely from his shoulders; and he raised his palm to them from the street almost as if he wanted to break their fall from the balcony.

Lorenza and Marta rushed to meet them in the entryway, but then when they saw Arturo they stopped short. The familiarity that they'd had with him as children didn't seem possible and they didn't know if they were supposed to hug him or greet him with a simple handshake. Just as he always had, Arturo thwarted all their plans and without saying a word he threw them into Margot's arms as if by now he was only an extra; a former leading man whose days as a star were over.

They had been expecting them for days and Isabella had prepared the table with a linen tablecloth and a bunch of cornflowers in the middle. And when Enrico arrived, they all went in to sit down near the radio and the questions flew back and forth with no room for answers. Arturo and Margot had to get back on the train in two hours and they couldn't even stay for lunch; they were going to Naples and then to Capri. "I'm sorry," Margot told her sister, "but we only have three days." "It doesn't matter, at least we got to see each other." The air that came in through the open window shone brightly in their wine goblets and Isabella seemed to be going over in her mind the gestures of spreading out the tablecloth and arranging the cornflowers in the center of the table; and then she had tilted her head a little to the side to see how it looked.

They had a lot of things to tell them about; too many, Margot said. They had been married only a week and Arturo had to go back to Trieste, where he was working as an interpreter for the Allied command. She set a little bag of candy favors on top of the radio and now Isabella was asking her if Trieste too had been destroyed and how much it cost to live there, if it was already hot there like it was in Rome. As if these were the most important things to know; and her eyes kept returning to Arturo's face almost as if she were searching for some detail that made it different from the way it used to be.

Margot was sitting in front of the window and the suit she had sewn from the cloth of a Royal Navy uniform was making her perspire. She had put on weight but beneath the stiff blue material one could still sense the wiry strength of her back and shoulders. Her eyes sparkled and her small hands, puffy from the night on the train and the heat moved to accompany her words as if she were running out of breath. Happy? Oh, yes, very much so. . . . After months of fear and deprivation, life seemed beautiful to her now. As soon as the war ended in May, without waiting even one more day, Arturo had *catapulted* (that's the word she used, *catapulted*) into Italy. He came across the border illegally without going through all of the bureaucracy necessary to get a visa stamped on his passport, and she joined him a few weeks later.

But Isabella seemed more interested in hearing about their new life together and she asked her again about Trieste as if she wanted to try to imagine where they lived, the pine trees and the blue of the sea, the cafés in the squares. She felt old, she said. Hunger, especially the implacable hunger of Lorenza and Marta, had forced her to make repeated trips to the 'pawnbroker's shop to pawn a ring or a bracelet, and then she had to walk for miles to get a kilo of sugar or a rabbit, or a jar of lard. She smiled and her aquiline nose stood out against the pallor of her skin where her big blue eyes gave off a light, pale glow. She got up to at least offer them some of the wine she had put on ice and as her hands took the glasses from the table-cloth, the reflection from all that white revealed the rouge on her cheekbones, the makeup powder moist from the heat. And that old age that she seemed to be joking about now became a shadow that was already spreading its tentacles around her lovely face. "The fear that something might happen to Enrico," she went on, "the start every time the doorbell rang"; her voice, slightly hoarse from the cigarettes she'd been smoking again, almost a monotone, life-less. But her daughters quickly interrupted her because it was bor-ing to keep on talking about the same old things while it was so much fun listening to Margot.

And Arturo? His mouth isn't the way it used to be. It's difficult to tell exactly what's changed, if it's the lips that are thinner or the teeth that have lost some of their gleam. In Trieste he always has to keep moving around from one command to another in a jeep with the sun beating down and dust blowing in everywhere. Never a minute's rest, he says, the leave time to get married granted at the last moment over objections from everyone; and now as Isabella hands him a glass, she can make out the wrinkles around his eyes, his now-short bristly hair where the gray hairs have multiplied, and her gaze loses itself in those irises so black they can't be distin-guished from his pupils. Something that she used to call *the color of your soul* and that allowed him to guard all his emotions so well.

Arturo has slipped the glass out of her hand almost without touching her, in an instant, and Isabella is already moving away, sit-ting down on the arm of the chair next to her sister who is recount-ing their wedding with the enthusiastic voice of an adolescent. De-spite the heat and that heavy wool suit, Margot seems to emanate a "sense of life." A different future, light and airy. Now Arturo adds his voice to that of his young wife and they describe the ceremony before the military chaplain, just the witnesses and the two officers that work in the same office with Arturo. "So you got married in church?" Isabella asked, amazed. "Margot really wanted to, I didn't care one way or another," he answered. Only then did Isabella seem to notice the wedding ring on his finger and her eyes stared at the thin circle of gold. "And the white dress? Weren't you sorry not to have even a white dress?" Lorenza asked. "Sorry? No. . . . This suit was just fine; I even wore a hat!" and her honey-brown eyes squeezed narrower between her eyelids to contain her joy. At the end of the summer they'll have to leave Trieste, she goes on, maybe they'll go to the United States; it depends on whether or not Arturo wants to go back to teaching at a university. "Would you come back to Rome then?" Isabella asked and her gaze left Arturo's hand to wander outside in the sky above the sun-yellowed walls. "To Rome, never" he answered; and his voice, though it was impossible to say why, sounded cruel.

Then Margot wanted to see the house. She took off her jacket and, despite the added weight, her body still had all its old agility, a sort of fervor that started in her shoulders and moved down through her smooth, thin forearms, all the way to her hands swollen from the heat. Isabella closed the shutters because the sun was becoming unbearable and together with her daughters she took her through the rooms. Arturo and Enrico were left alone in the half-light that clung warmly to the velvet flowers on the reclining chair; and Enrico told the story of his first encounter with Signora Arnitz many years ago. The scandal because her daughter was marrying a simple teacher whose career was still uncertain; and Arturo laughed. That sound so similar to the sound of the past reached the girls and Isabella on their tour of the rooms like a signal announcing the return to the normalcy of their days. Of their days *once upon a time*.

But when Enrico decided to bring Arturo up to date on everything that had happened at the institute during his absence, about the others who, like him, had been forced out of teaching by reason of race, Arturo cut him off: "I already know everything" he said, "But I knew *almost* everything before." He got up and looked out

94

through the half-open shutters down onto the faded awning over the general store, the half erased, semicircular sign in front of the garage, "I don't think I could bear to see Pende again, or 'Pupilli the faithful,' " he said suddenly. And he told how in Trieste, at the Allied command, it was easy to obtain information because the Americans had huge collections of documents. Enrico looked at his slightly curved back in that oversized jacket and now that he was Margot's husband he felt like he was seeing him with new eyes, less enchanted. "But are you allowed to consult them?" he asked, "I've heard it's very difficult." "Not for me, I help them in some of the research. I'm always running into names like Buffarini Guidi, Visco, Ussani, Pende. But really they didn't count for anything, they were only Limbo." He had emptied his glass and he was filling it again, his hand tight around the neck of the bottle. "Imagine the consequences of the racial laws enforced to the hilt. In all the occupied countries, practically in almost all of Europe." But he stopped himself there because Margot and Isabella had come back and Isabella was opening the piano, taking the felt off the keys. "Why don't you play something for us?" she asked, bowing her head as her lips made way for that old captivating smile. No, he didn't feel like it. He hadn't played since he left; he was totally out of practice he said. He came closer and with just one finger, like a beginner, tapped out on the keys the notes to *Rosamundo*, almost as if he wanted to hear the sound of that piano again, just for a minute.

But Margot and Enrico didn't take to each other. As often happened to him with people he didn't know well, when Enrico tried to talk to her the words struggled to fall from his lips, almost ceremoniously. Now Margot was leaning with her arms against the back of Arturo's chair and her hands softly caressed the back of his neck as her modulated voice joined those of Isabella and the girls. It dominated them. A voice tempered by singing, warm and just slightly weary; and now and again Enrico would look at her almost as if to ask himself what had made Arturo, once so diffident toward marriage, marry that girl who never stopped flashing those beautiful golden eyes, who was always so confident and self-assured. Qualities which signaled in no uncertain terms her "provenance"; that not even the hard years, which Margot called the *clandestine years*, had been able to crack.

She was too much taken with her love affair to notice anything. "Isn't it all so wonderful?" she seemed to be saying as her breast brushed up against her husband's bristly hair, perspiration marks showing on the underarms of her blouse and her body happily abandoned against the back of the armchair. Arturo was finally showing some signs that he had noticed Lorenza and Marta too and he was joking now about the coating of lipstick he had discovered on their mouths. Shame, shame, shame, he said, the love for his new bride visibly clouding his mind. His strong hand, darkened by the sun, took hold of Lorenza's face and squeezed till it hurt, his eyes scrutinizing with feigned severity her overly painted lips, the rosy cheeks of that little girl who was so wild about American chocolate bars and Carnation powdered milk. Films with Gary Cooper. Lorenza blushed and tried to look away from the blackness of those suddenly stern eyes.

The war has been over for just two weeks and even though they're poor and all patched up, their faces thinned out (even Isabella, even her clothes are too big for her), they are all free to love each other and imagine a future for themselves. Everything can begin again in the creaking of the seats of the darkened cinemas where those gigantic close-ups, with their impalpable light and shadows, pierce through the clouds of smoke above the crowd. In the great piazzas come back to life with waving colored flags, sewn together the night before, and loud speakers croaking out from above the stage the new songs of freedom. Everyone free to decorate their lapels with ivy, the hope of a republic still waiting to be born, or an obstinate Savoy knot, symbol of the monarchy. To take to the streets with their enthusiasm or with their anger in pursuit of the infamous. Everyone can resume the thread of their lives at the point where it had broken off, and those who had never "been with" someone, like that young girl who rubs her cheeks with geranium petals to give them color, can choose among the vast range of possibilities their very own King of Hearts.

A morning that ends in glory among the candy favors opened one after another, smooth outside and hard inside, the squeal of a jeep taking a curve. The bells of Piazza del Popolo are starting to play the Angelus and Margot's hands slide down from Arturo's head as she straightens herself up, throwing her hair back in that way her suitors used to love. "God, how late it is," she says, a rumpled flower from her wedding bouquet still in her pocket.

She was pregnant but she hadn't told anyone but Isabella; and before leaving the two of them went off to talk privately. They lingered together in the bedroom where the mullion-framed mirrors flickered in the half-light. A great understanding seemed to have been reborn between the two sisters, thanks to Arturo, and Isabella made her a present of her embroidered tulle scarf from Venice. But when Margot's and Arturo's voices had faded away in the stairwell, Isabella started to cry and Enrico pretended not to see her tears. Lorenza and Marta ran out onto the balcony to wave good-bye one last time and saw the two of them walking arm in arm like Mamma, Papa, and Arturo used to do. Before disappearing into Piazzale Flaminio, Margot turned and waved her hand in farewell, her lips saying something the girls couldn't understand. Then with broad gestures they asked, *what, what did you say?* And Margot repeated it, syllable by syllable. But they shook their heads; they didn't understand. Then Arturo pulled his young bride away, the train for Naples would soon be pulling into the station, scorching hot on the tracks. And a truck, bouncing along over the tram tracks, suddenly hid them from view.

PART 2

1

The euphoria of the summer of '45 gave way almost immediately to a sense of bewilderment in a situation where *after* was continually mixed up with *before*, as if life, still imbued with so much uncertainty and hardship, were moving ahead by jolts and bounces on those torn up roads full of gaping holes, uprooted bridges, rubble. That's when the Days of the Young Girls really began.

From one season to the next their breasts stretched the buttons on their blouses and lifted the wool of their sweaters, their legs finally lost their bony ungainliness and filled out even a little too much below the hems of their skirts. They learned how to use a comb and kept lipstick in their shoulder bags, determined to overcome all their fears if someone should try to pick them up out on the street. But it was also an overflowing of feelings, longings, eruptions of bad moods and cheerfulness, voices and desires joined together in a continually expanding magma, uncontainable within the walls of the house. Even the piano, thumped at the most unthinkable hours of the day, became part of that impetuous and insatiable monster-body, whose features were in continual transformation. Every corner of the house, every hour of the day was now threatened by its potential expansion, dressed in the sweet, bright colors of youth, its uncontrollable range of sounds. Isabella felt nearly paralyzed by it, powerless to slow its advance. And although Marta, along with her myopic, sky-blue eyes, had inherited a certain Nordic composure, Lorenza was a savage antagonist, with her sharp voice and rapid-fire gesticulation.

The first signs appeared some time later, barely noticeable (but afterward it was almost impossible to establish exactly *when*); and immediately Isabella put them behind her. She, who had never liked to scrutinize or probe herself, observing in the mirror the groove of the circles under her eyes or the steady advance of gray hairs, tried not to think about those pains that came on suddenly like lances jabbing the middle of her back and then faded over the course of several hours until they were forgotten. Shadows, rifts, that plunged into her day like little vessels of darkness. Negligible little signs that marked the passage from one age to another, from the light of maturity to the chiaroscuro of "then." The ineluctable then.

The following years brought the trips to Switzerland, to Geneva, Zurich, and Interlaken. The brief visits to Mamigna who was never told the real reason for all that moving around from place to place. A recognized disease, certified by the incontrovertible evidence illuminated by the bluish glow of the negatives held up against the light, confirmed by the decimal figures of the blood tests. Their hopes growing dimmer each time; and then, suddenly, the final surrender.

Interminable months. But later those same months seemed incredibly short, a parenthesis, the passage from one paragraph to another that marked time in black margins. Everything that happened up to the day of the funeral, when Marta and Lorenza knelt beside their father in Santa Maria del Popolo, suddenly began to fade away with dizzying velocity. They didn't even know anymore if it had been a happy time or an unhappy one, all they knew was that the road ahead seemed suddenly deserted and the horizon appeared as an indistinct series of points: cupolas, bell towers, trees, hills reduced to profiles cut out against the great void of the sky.

The inevitable falling out between Lorenza and Marta came right away. Loving her mother with an adoration that managed, like the stomach of an ostrich, to digest all errors and defects, Marta had always made life difficult for her sister. In this respect she resembled her father. Enrico too accepted the good and the bad from his wife as the inseparable components of a whole whose name was Isabella: breath, voice, melancholy and cheerfulness, expectations that held back the boredom. And as long as she remained at his side the force of that feeling made him into a rock, invulnerable to any kind of attack. Now he was a caged animal. One of those proud ones that pace back and forth between two fake caves, pretending that the zoo is the jungle, sullenly indifferent to the visitors crowding around the fence waiting for a show that will never take place.

But while Marta was still groping around for her bowl of milk, Lorenza wanted the streets and the trees, the *others*. The give and take of stimulating conversation, unexpected friendships born under the cupola of an umbrella. Outside the exit of the cinema. Studying with fingers ruffling through hair and eyes aflame over a book; and then putting on a colorful dress and a new pair of shoes and slamming the door closed on leaving the house. Going out on the streets still hot from the sun without any precise destination, talking and laughing with a group of friends. Listening to the latest recording of the New Orleans Jazz Band and the piano of Irving Berlin, his voice singing *Blue Skies*. Or the one like the screech of a dragonfly that belongs to Ella Fitzgerald. And slouched in an armchair she let her eyes follow the smoke of the cigarette held lightly between her index and middle fingers (such is the look, the gesture, of someone gathering herself together to roam freely, one day, out in the world).

Almost a loathing for the presence of Marta who, like a bird, carries her worm of suffering around with her. Sometimes she catches a glimpse of her lying on the double bed waiting, amid the glittering reflections of the mirrors, for the bittersweet taste of memories to come forth from the shadows and visit her. Even the most insignificant ones, the ones that seem lost in her memory and that Marta cunningly tries to recover, casting her glance over the colors, the changing light, the objects that day after day through the years had composed her love story with her mother.

A comedy which Lorenza refuses to be part of, there is no suitable role for her. Her father and Marta have taken it all for themselves; and so she rebels, screams, she can't stand this playacting. She had a boyfriend at the time; he was about to take his degree in architecture and he took her around Rome on the back of his motorbike. He showed her Bramante's façades, the courtyard of Palazzo Spada, where her gaze lost itself in the illusionary perspective of Borromini's gallery. They went for walks along the orange tree–bordered footpaths on the Aventine Hill and talked and talked, the soles of their shoes crunching in the gravel. And they kept on talking with their elbows leaning on the parapet, looking out on the horizon that seemed to break through the background of roof tiles and cupolas and stretch out into the parched colors of the twilight. Far away, all the way to the countryside, shimmering with thorn bushes and low-lying hills. Wavering slightly, the boy's fingers point out the façades of the churches amid the pasty yellow of the roof tiles, his shirt open at the neck, his mouth closer and closer, his words as if they were colored: ochre, purple, orange. Gray violet. Dogs running free off their leashes.

The wonder of being not yet twenty, Isabella has been dead for just a few months and all of a sudden the boy asks her: why don't we get married? He has fallen in love with her, wants her with him forever. In love? Lorenza laughs, get a load of this guy, a few extra caresses and he's lost his head. He wants to marry her. Are you crazy? No, he's not crazy, he loves her. Lorenza squints to stare at that massive face whose beard always casts a bluish shadow over its pale cheeks; one of his front teeth is chipped. It happened when he fell from a window, he said, escaping from the Fascists. Lorenza has never decided whether that face is handsome or ugly, if that chipped tooth is a fault or a mark of glory. So will you? She's turned around as if she had to look for the answer on some bench or in some tree behind her. The boy has longingly leaned his face against her neck; to you my forehead, my eyelashes, my bristly chin whose beard rebels against the razor. His lips skim warmly over the little bit of bare skin that emerges from her dress, his body pressed against hers. A man is looking at them, he's stocky, with a gray jacket and dusty shoes. "Yes, okay," she answers in a rush, "but you go tell my father about it."

This way she could get away from that house creaking in the emptiness of the night like a ship riding at anchor. She would be done with all that mourning, Marta's submissive weeping. Her unbearable sodality with their father's pain.

But to put her life in order Lorenza would have to have a clear conscience, only then would she be able to look back and erase some features in favor of others, recover the frame where Isabella has her fine and thin blond curls and her birdlike profile lying on the pillow. Her eyelid light as a leaf in her sunken eye socket, the dark gray shadows on her cheeks damp with fever. A beauty the disease has attacked but not managed to destroy.

Recover the happiness of that gesture when her mother would throw her scarf around her neck or open the keyboard of the piano to pick out a melody on the keys, her voice humming the notes of some music heard who knows where, or when. Grasp the meaning of those profound silences, total, that covered over several points in her life as if it were a chessboard and Isabella, queen or bishop, incapable of the surprise jump of the knight. Now the chessboard was deformed, there was no longer any order among the squares, no more bishops or queens, or even any kings castled in the corners, behind them a barren land open to incursions while the question of *what happened to her* presented itself as a place that was dangerous to venture into without the proper equipment.

There were no letters tied together with yellow or lavender (her favorite color) silk ribbons, nor any secret boxes. She had always glued her pictures of Enrico and her daughters into cloth photo albums, writing in lovely calligraphy the year and the place in which they were taken. The others she let pile up in the top drawer of her dresser, together with her handkerchiefs and gloves. Disorderly Isabella; pictures of Alberto similar to the ones lined up on the mantel over the fireplace at Chesa Silvascina and still others of Alberto's wedding at Villa d'Este, where her young big brother is all spit and polish in his tuxedo and his bride looks like she's about to take flight, the long train of her dress sliding down the steps, while she, Isabella, is a skinny young girl with glasses, wearing a ridiculous looking bridesmaid's dress. Just one picture of Mamigna on the arm of her first husband, that "Papi" from whom Alberto had gotten his passion for travel and of whom she, Isabella, if she hadn't had the picture, wouldn't even have remembered his face. A "Papi" with a round Swiss beard who nurtured more than a few doubts about the paternity of his second child.

In the picture he has his arm around Mamigna in front of a Chesa Silvascina still under construction. Mamigna is small and thin at his side and the house is showing off its skeleton of wood beams surrounded by big piles of sand. There's a cement mixer in one corner and a big empty space in the foreground where the swimming pool would be. A few years later they would separate and Isabella would receive only scanty reports of her presumed father; up until that accidental death on the road going up to Mt. Grossglockner. Just one picture of Margot, too, standing in the garden of her house in Providence, Rhode Island. Margot is smiling just slightly as she holds up to the photographer a small child all bundled up in a snowsuit. She holds him tight against her chest so his face, half submerged under a wool beret, will be in the center of the frame. The baby carriage with its blankets all jumbled up beside them.

Rose is a rose is a rose is a rose. Creeping plants with soft flowers climb up the gates of town cemeteries and there is always a grave-digger who makes the gravel crunch carrying a bunch of keys on his belt. A thin, haggard grave-digger, or a flabby one with baggy pants. But for the very young, death has the wings of the dragonfly. Invisible in flight, it fascinates and repels with its odor of myrtle and the corroded tombstones with the barely legible writing behind the wilted flowers. And even when it explodes like a dove hit in midflight, bones and feathers are quickly recomposed in a haphazard fashion in homage to a future that is still so largely over-abundant. Only much later, after years have gone by, can one see the crudeness and haste with which those fragments were reassembled to await the day they would be finally filed away.

Only when Lorenza felt herself to be her mother sitting on a bench (just as she had seen her so many times, her blue overcoat unbuttoned and her big white hands folded across her purse), sitting there with her melancholy and her distraction, her gaze lost in the clawing feet of a blackbird and boredom, like dust, coating her blond hair. Only then did Isabella present herself again with urgency and the unanswered questions begin to move like crazed pawns across a chessboard without any more distinctions between the black squares and the white. The Moviola quickly rewound the film whose images had been spinning through it for such a long time and brought it to a halt at the very first frame: that triangle at the far end of the dining room where *she* has dandruff on her dress and laughs throwing her head back, her round hips pressing against the rigid back of the armchair.

Start over again from there; or even earlier, from those blank spaces that she left behind her. The ones she intended to be that way; and others too that had, so to speak, dissolved themselves in memory.

Lorenza began with the house in Mendrisio. With that little house similar to so many others built at the beginning of the century and then modified over time with new stucco, new shutters, add-on terraces with views of the lake. In front of the house was the lawn where as a little girl Isabella had watched her older brother show off with his daredevil games. The swing suspended between two iron poles where he flew high standing on the center board, propelled by the thrust of his body. And she had grown up there with Alberto, they laughed and played and fought together; up until Mamigna's second marriage.

Then Lorenza decided to go to see Montreux and the high school where first her brother and then Isabella had studied. She sat in the café in the square looking around at the tables, trying to understand which one the young Isabella might have chosen the afternoon that she met the man who was to become her husband. A young school teacher who had come to Montreux in response to an announcement of openings for foreign teachers. Like her she ordered a slice of cake, and imagined the flowerpots full of pansies, the last gasps of winter reluctantly giving way to spring.

That day Mamma had worn a scarf and a red beret; later on Papà adored her scarves, even after she put on weight and her blue over-coat marked her hips. He had just taken his degree in mathematics; she hated everything that had anything to do with numbers and didn't trust Italians. But suddenly Italy seemed like a marvelous place to her, full of interesting men and works of art that absolutely had to be seen. And despite the scarf that the gusty wind kept throwing up around her face, Enrico saw her as a girl unique in all the world, poetic and beautiful, unhappy because of an adverse destiny that he would overcome.

But that trip to Montreux was only a first step. Afterward, through Mamigna, Lorenza looked for other information, other addresses. But Signora Arnitz's memory had crumbled like an old wall and the addresses in her lilac-colored notebook were almost all out of date, the telephone numbers unlisted, and the people un-known, moved, or dead. Marisetta came to visit her every once in a while, but Marisetta had married a rich and respectable English gentleman and was living in the Devonshire countryside together with three children and two dogs. She answered Lorenza's letter with a note in bad Italian that gave no indication of a desire to see her. She wouldn't know what to say to her, she wrote, she had only seen Isabella a few times and she hardly remembered her, too much time had passed. And as for the others (and surely she meant Margot), if Mamigna hadn't given her the address she couldn't imagine who else could. Maybe the only person who could still help her was the old custodian from Chesa Silvascina.

And so, although rather reluctantly, Lorenza found her way to Margot. But it wasn't easy. After several months in Trieste, Margot and Arturo had moved to the United States, where their son was born. A child with a malformed heart who lived just a few, hellish months. And then Arturo emigrated to Israel and she came back to Europe. In fact they had separated although legally they continued for some time to be husband and wife. Her tracks formed a kind of zigzag itinerary: France, Italy, then again to the south of France and a brief stay in the Pyrenees. Then the little flag with Margot written on it suddenly disappeared, and the information about her dwindled down to uncertain suppositions.

Actually, Margot had planted her flag not far from those lakes whose shores her suitor from Zurich had pedaled along on his bike from Saint Moritz. For the first time she bought a house; nothing at all like Chesa Silvascina, just some old stone farmhouse walls. Two rooms plus a barn that she converted into a workshop with one large wooden loom and two smaller ones. In her letter to Lorenza she described the place and how to get there, the blankets woven by hand from wool that she tinted herself with vegetable dyes (that was her most appreciated work, she said, and in the summertime she hung them outside her door, managing to sell them without going through the stores in Saint Moritz and Pontresina). But she preferred working on pillows, squares with minute patterns where she had the sense of weaving together patches of sky with foliage from the trees, just as they looked to her from the little window in her workshop, high up and wedged into the thick walls. The same window that the cows had contemplated in the old days, lifting their heads from the trough.

The reference to the cows irritated Lorenza. It brought back to her as if in an echo the enthusiastic voice of the young woman recounting her postwar wedding. But on the day she arrived, she found waiting for her a woman with gray hair cut short on her round head, a sort of shearing that brought out her eyes, still limpid and moist between her dark eyelashes. Otherwise Margot looked more like a farm woman than Arturo's young wife who had come to visit her sister just after the war. Thick woolen socks protected her feet inside her clogs and her bust swelled her dark cotton dress into a uniform bulge. She welcomed Lorenza with great simplicity, inviting her to stay. If you'd like to stay, she said, I'd be happy to have you. A few days, a week, or even longer. Lorenza would just have to get used to the noise of the loom. She worked at night and the bedroom was next to the workshop. As far as she was concerned, there was nothing to worry about, she added, there was a couch next to the loom and she almost always slept there. "I like the smell of the wool," she said, "that way even while I'm sleeping I remember where I am."

Later on Lorenza sat down in front of the window that had been opened up onto the valley; from there one could see the stream cut like a knife through the long green slope and the road following it for a stretch and then crossing over it in a sharp curve, white with dust. Some hikers were walking down it at a determined pace while some children ran ahead, shaking the boards of the little wooden bridge. "Did Mamma ever come here?" she asked. "I don't think so; when she was young she would never have gone so far away from Chesa Silvascina. She didn't like to go hiking."

Margot came over to sit near her and her small, wrinkled fingers rested lightly on the bench. They were worn from work and time but they still showed the delicacy that had always been in contrast with her athletic body. Even now, as Lorenza sensed the heavy weight of her body on the bench, the lightness of her hands seemed to extend to her smooth, thin forearms. Lorenza felt the desire to touch them, but as though she had read her mind, Margot pulled them back under her armpits.

Outside, along the road, the adults had caught up to the children on the bridge and they were hanging over it to look down at the water as it thrashed up against the rocks, their colorful rucksacks on their backs. It would be dark soon and when the first lights came on in the houses scattered among the meadows Margot would take down the blankets hanging outside the door, folding them up one by one on the wooden shelves. Just as she had been doing for years and would continue to do without ever asking herself how long it would go on, the big photograph of Alberto submerging slowly into the darkness. A photograph left intact over the years with the ski tips crossed against the eternal blue of the sky. "That's the only thing I wanted to keep when Chesa Silvascina was sold," she said. "So then it's not true that you hated him?" "Who? Alberto? Why should I have hated him?" And in a flash Lorenza recalled when as a child she had concentrated on Mamma's presence almost as if the force of thought could keep her for just another minute in the doorway where her figure was framed big and blond, her face already erased by the darkness. In the same way now, mentally, without moving, she wanted to hold on to that vision of the slope, those children still standing on the bridge as the clouds came and went in large shadowy patches over the meadows. She was finally there, where she *had to get to*, where with her gradually waning strength she wanted to be *before it was too late*.

Afterward, while they were preparing dinner together, Lorenza watched her as she moved slowly and calmly around the kitchen: a woman who, together with the worship of memories, seemed to

have banished all traces of feminine vanity. And yet she was still seductive. Maybe it was in those barely visible outlines of her figure,
marks left on the canvas from a working sketch that no paint ever
manages to eliminate altogether. In the almost identical Margots
like those wooden Russian dolls that always have a new one inside;
right down to the last one, the one that won't open, the hard nut
inside its shell. Doll halves thrown into a corner like boxes without their tops; the Margot in the dirndl and the one in the chalet
with her hands warm from the fire, lying on the pillows on the
floor. The Margot that Eddy is taking pictures of; she laughs and
insults him and the suitor who's pedaled up on his bicycle with the
newspapers in his basket is talking about General Guisan. Mamigna pours more tea in the sky-blue patterned cups and the sun
goes down behind the larch trees. Goose bumps raise the fine hair
on her forearms, I'm cold, she says, I'm going in to get a sweater. . . .

"But that time at Chesa Silvascina you said you hated Alberto,"
Lorenza said suddenly. Margot laughs, what a strange woman you
are, Lorenza, history is a fish inside an aquarium, it comes and goes
right before your eyes but you can never reach out and grab it. You
can only fantasize about how it might have been in the past, but
nothing else, nothing else. . . . Who knows why she said that that
day; maybe she was just offended because Isabella hadn't waited to
see her.

Now she was the "blanket woman," *die Bettdeckenfrau*. The one
that has planted her flag on a patch of ground where the dyed fabrics sway in the wind on sunny mornings. A woman of composed
gestures who never bargains over prices and silently folds up the
sold blankets, wrapping them up in large sheets of coffee-colored
paper, and in the evening she sits on the bench to watch the last
groups of hikers pass by down the road suddenly white in the
darkness. The same woman that during the night, like the weaver
in the fable, rapidly manipulates the wool threads to the brisk beat
of the spool as if the fabric growing in her hands will someday

bring her salvation; and then suddenly the house is silent. The Margot without dogs, without cats, without flowers, who fills the copper vases with pine branches, the only fragrance that she likes to smell in her rooms.

In the United States, when the crisis between her and Arturo seemed to be irresolvable, she tried to write down some notes to trace the path of her life and help her understand. But then she ripped them up because everything, as soon as it was written down, ended up sounding false. Starting with that telephone call in January '44, when with her hand on the receiver she had defended from all possible listeners the words that sank like daggers into Mamigna's heart.

She was in Coira that day, and Doctor Zurhaus had found her and Arturo a room in the house of an old patient of his. Doctor Zurhaus had lied; he and Arturo had never met in Paris or anywhere else (*I've also written a letter to Doctor Zurhaus*, Isabella had written), but as soon as he saw Arturo he embraced him. And after a brief moment of uncertainty for a welcome he hadn't expected, Arturo leaned his head on his delicate shoulder and cried, the doctor comforting him with little pats on the back. He knew, he said, about the work Arturo had done in Nice, and he wished he could help him much more, have him stay with him at his home, but the police had been keeping an eye on him for some time now because of the little he did to help the refugees.

That evening Margot opened up their suitcase on two chairs because nothing else fit in their room except the bed (but wasn't that what she desired more than anything else, a bed in which to lie in each other's arms and feel each other's bodies during the night?). Doctor Zurhaus came back later on and turned the radio dial to a station that broadcast classical music. He sat there listening with his eyes closed, his eyelids like dried petals and his hands folded over his vest with the gold watch chain, almost a small scale reproduction of himself, so much had the years eaten away at the insides of the little doctor with the white hair, leaving intact only his proportions; his clean, perfect shirt, his polished shoes, and the small starched white shirt cuffs.

A telltale cat smell drifted through the house; but maybe it was just the onions cooking in a dented aluminum pan. Afterward, when the music was over and they had eaten the onion soup, the doctor told them that for some time now he had been in contact with a colleague in Zurich, Doctor Bucher, who during a trip to Eastern Europe had come to know what was really happening there. The real nature of the tasks assigned to the *Einsatzgruppen*. What Hitler meant by the solution to the Jewish Question. *Endlösung*, he said, lowering his eyelids as if he had to cover up the shame of that word, and then *Judenrein*. Two aseptic terms that meant horror and death for thousands, hundreds of thousands of men and women. And children. Maybe more, Arturo said, certainly a lot more, we'll never know how many of us were taken (for the first time he had said "us" and Margot looked at him surprised). *Judenrein*, he went on to explain, meant the total cleansing of the Jews, like mopping the floor, it means that as soon as they're killed they burn them in ovens so there's nothing left but a handful of ashes. And in the face of Margot's disbelief, Doctor Zurhaus cited Tertullian: *Credo quia absurdum*. Although, he added, Tertullian meant it in a completely different way.

That night Arturo sank into a cataleptic sleep and for the first time they didn't make love; she cried. She felt herself suffocating in that cramped room; foolish, desperate tears wetting her pillow.

After that Doctor Zurhaus came by every night and each time he sat and listened to the music with his eyes closed. But then some of the neighbors began to take an interest in Arturo, in that couple who appeared from time to time behind the window panes. They started asking questions. Too many, the alarmed landlady said one night to

Doctor Zurhaus. And finally the doctor himself advised them to hurry up and close their suitcase and get on the first train. After some uncertainty, despite the distance, the choice had fallen on Fribourg, where Doctor Zurhaus had some safe friends and where it would be easier to pass unobserved. The doctor then decided to board the train together with them and he chatted cheerfully during the whole trip never showing an instant of apprehension, sitting straight and stiff as if he were wearing armor; and his eyes enlarged by his glasses challenged the conductor hanging over him with his heavy shoulder bag. Profoundly candid as he lied. And if the conductor had more than a doubt that Arturo was his son, he didn't dare insist, his big bag swaying back and forth with the rocking of the train and just brushing by the small white head. (*His deep religious sense*, Isabella had written, *his "preserved innocence" which is innocence extended to a painful experience of the world*.)

Once they'd arrived in Fribourg the doctor accompanied them on their search for a place that was safe and at the same time suitable for their scarce financial resources. When he left Margot embraced him, and against the fullness of her body she felt all the frailty and emptiness of his, almost as if by now Doctor Zurhaus consisted only of the heavy dark wool of his suit.

In Fribourg, Arturo continued writing letter after letter in the hope of obtaining a residence permit and a food ration card. The much desired and denied "*Urlaub.*" Margot mailed them for him when she went to work in the morning at a photo workshop. Letters addressed to Lausanne and Geneva. But also to France; and those were the most important but also the least likely to reach their destination.

It was Eddy's passion for everything related to film and lenses, his continuous playing around with developing acids and fixing solutions, that allowed Margot to get the job in that workshop. So many times, locked in the bathroom at Chesa Silvascina, they had printed negatives with their heads pressed together waiting for the miracle of the image to emerge from the water, the slightly satanic light of the red bulb hanging from the wire shining on their ghostly faces. Now what had seemed like a hobby turned out to be very useful, and with the help of a printer friend of Doctor Zurhaus, Margot had even succeeded in "making up" a false document for Arturo. A *biffe* as he called it; and every morning with the *biffe* in his pocket he went to the library where he could finally be warm and have access to all the books he always wanted to read.

But then the photo workshop closed down and Margot found a job as a waitress in the restaurant at the Hôtel de Fribourg. And though the work was harder it was also more varied. She enjoyed herself passing among the tables making all those gestures she had seen Lula make, smiling when she poured the wine or bent down with the serving tray balanced on her hand, or waited to receive payment of the bill, pulling out the change from a small purse hidden under her apron. She was flattered by the men's glances as she moved swiftly and directly from one side of the room to the other, and then pushed open the spring-loaded door to the kitchen with a swift kick. Sometimes one of the customers would ask how she spent her free nights, as his glance moved up from her ankles to her knee, trying to guess the length of her thighs under her skirt.

That was their best time together. She was making more money and they were able to leave that seedy pension where Doctor Zurhaus had set them up for another one where they turned on the heat in the afternoons. When Arturo went to the library in the mornings and nothing and nobody reminded him what it meant to be Jewish, he experienced a kind of exaltation. For the first time he could feel the loosening of the vise that had made him into a "conscious pariah" and he stopped to look at the window displays, smiling at the salesgirl on the other side of the glass. He would go into the bookstores and mingle with the people leafing through the books, linger in front of the newspaper stand. He even stopped tormenting himself about the fate of all those who were left behind in France or Italy and it was Margot, when she came home in the evening, who gave him the latest news on the advance of the Russians or the proclamations of the Republic of Salò.

But as the weeks went by the librarian also started giving him a kind of bulletin on the war. She was a tall, horsey woman with a colorless face and two small shiny cheekbones. She had taken a liking to him and sometimes in the afternoon, when they were alone, she offered him tea and biscuits. From the very first day she called him *Herr Professor* and addressed him with high regard. *Ordentlicher Professor*? she asked him one morning as she walked over to the table where he was reading. *Geshichtsprofessor*, he specified, smiling over the top of his book. From that day on, every time he asked for a title, she would ask him why, and Arturo invented an improbable research project on a mathematical formula that would explain the recurrence in different eras of events such as persecution or regicide. Famine. This only added to her esteem and this fiction soon turned out to be very useful for the request of all kinds of books. And slowly everything that was happening beyond the barbed wire barriers separating Switzerland from the rest of the world started to fade away. To break off like something going off on its own, adrift on the current while he stood there on the beach watching. A shipwreck survivor, nothing more than a survivor who had saved his skin despite everything and everybody.

After a while the librarian got into the habit of putting a chocolate bar next to his book, one of the ones with the view of Switzerland on the label, because she had understood that he was having a hard time getting enough food and those biscuits that she offered him with the tea vanished in an instant. She would stop for a minute, pleased to watch him eat it, piece by piece, as he kept on reading. But one afternoon when Arturo slipped the bar into his pocket she came over to him and asked him, with a strange smile on her face, if he was saving it for someone. "Vielleicht für Ihr Mädchen," she added. "Mein Mädchen?" Yes, she had seen him one afternoon walking arm-in-arm along the Sarine with a girl. A very lovely young woman, she said, and her voice sounded as though she were making an effort not to seem inquisitorial. Then Arturo felt afraid again, it even seemed to him that when she passed by his overcoat hanging from a hook she had looked at the lining to see the label.

So he started going to the library less often. Every time she saw him come in the librarian would get all nervous and her cheeks would turn fiery red. Maybe she's simply fallen in love with you, Margot said. Maybe; but that didn't change anything. Even a slightly more careful check and his document would be revealed for what it was, an amateurish fake. He had seen a lot of false documents, he had spent months making them and he used to travel around with a German "*Ausweis*" that was a perfect reproduction. But anyone could tell that the one he had in his pocket now was the first and probably the only experiment of a novice.

In the end he didn't go at all anymore and if he wanted some books Margot would go and get them from a small lending library. Whatever she could find; most of the time books that bored him and he would end up spending the whole day in bed, wrapped up in every piece of clothing he had, waiting for her to come home so they could make love. And while they embraced and rolled around among the clothes still scattered among the blankets, he would eat whatever she'd brought him from the Hôtel de Fribourg. His fingers all greasy; those caresses, those embraces that tasted of mutton and strudel.

They did it constantly as if Arturo had transferred his hunger and tension into the expectation of those embraces, and the hunger and tension could only be placated by her body. But when the nice weather arrived Arturo started going outside again to go and wait for her outside the Hôtel de Fribourg for her afternoon break. They looked at each other and smiled at a distance; and once her colleagues from work had gone their separate ways, they would take shelter inside a doorway to kiss. That was the longest kiss of the day; *the kiss of heart* they called it.

But that too turned out to be very imprudent and they had to change cities in a big rush. They decided on Lausanne. In Lausanne was the headquarters of Délivrance, the largest of the refugee assistance organizations, and Lausanne was also where Angelo Donati had taken refuge. He was a wealthy Italian Jew who, in Nice, had managed to save thousands of other Jews trapped in Nazi-occupied France. If he could only manage to contact him directly, Arturo was sure that he would be able to get a regular *Urlaub*.

After applying for jobs as a salesgirl in various stores, Margot was now the cashier at the Confiserie Belle-Fontaine. At the beginning she found it difficult with her small hands to pick up the coins from the counter; but she quickly learned how to slide them across the marble and then pick them up with the tips of her fingernails. And though the work was more monotonous than her previous jobs, the store had a nice smell of toasted almonds and Mademoiselle Janton looked like one of her fondants, always dressed in lilac or light pink.

Every day Margot stopped at the post office near Rue Deville and one evening she came home waving in her hand the answer that Arturo had been expecting for months. It wasn't what he had been hoping for; but the next day he went anyway to the office of Délivrance to see if they might be able to help him somehow. He walked around for a long time trying to find Place Palud and then he had to wait his turn in an anteroom where it was impossible to breathe from the bad breath and the smell. Finally the secretary to whom he had given his copious file told him that the way things stood there wasn't much hope; first he would have to turn himself in. But Arturo would never do that, he considered it too risky.

He left with the Délivrance newsletter in his pocket. For the moment that was all he could get. It was the end of the working day and the store windows were starting to light up. A blue light was rising up from the lake and the tram glided swiftly along the tracks with the passengers sitting like mannequins, the last rays of sunlight dissolving high up in the mountains still white with snow. A harsh spring, colorless, that showed itself only in the change of light, impalpable and airy. In the jingling of hundreds of bicycle bells. He came to the Confiserie Belle-Fontaine and from the window he could see Margot sitting at the cash register in her black smock with the white lace collar, all combed and composed like a prep school girl. And together with a great wave of tenderness he felt an immeasurable sadness, a sudden void of desire as if it were all fake and useless. Suffering, escaping, wanting at all costs to survive.

At home he wanted to make love all night long. But Margot had worked all day, she was tired, and she fell asleep wrapped in the blankets. He kept on kissing her and caressing her receiving in exchange only a sleepy smile, more a grimace than anything else, as she turned to the other side. She just didn't feel like waking up. So Arturo curled up in a corner of the bed, his eyes fixed on the light from the street as it reverberated on the ceiling. A desperation that even if she had forced herself to wake up, Margot would never have been able to understand.

It was the breath of all those people in the waiting room at Délivrance, but not only that. The silence of the children sitting on the bench against the wall, the women bundled up in the most disparate kinds of clothing. In an instant his brain went through all of the operations necessary to recompose piece by piece their miserable wandering. As if they were the same women and children outside the Hôtel Bompard in Marseilles under the boiling hot sun in the summer of '42.

2

Damned memory. How is it that memory can take one so far away
from what he has right before his eyes? From the springtime light
along the lakeshore drive and the festive jingling of all those bicycles; far away from Margot's face sticking out from under the
sheet, her breath warm with sleep? Bring back in a flash that morning of August '42, when at seven o'clock he turned the corner from
the still deserted Canebière and found himself in front of a police
line blocking the entrance to the Hôtel Bompard?

Up to that day he had never worried about anything else except
safeguarding his own "half-breed" self, careful to have all of his
documents so he could pass for a non-Jew. Make sure he had an
Ausweis every time he had to move from one zone to another. That
had been his main objective ever since he had left Italy for the second time in '41; and with the help of the dean of the school of medicine in Paris he'd managed again to get a position in Marseilles in
the "marine phytoculture" laboratory. He had no intention of con-
cerning himself with anything else; what was happening to him already seemed enough of an injustice without going around looking
for other problems. He had never been interested in politics; and if
he had been asked in the past to express his sympathies he would
have declared himself to be much more a conservative than a revo-
lutionary, a moderate supporter of liberal theories. Even with regard to music he and Enrico had always been traditionalists with a
decided preference for composers from the past as opposed to con-
temporaries like Schönberg or Alban Berg. The top place on his list
of interests was occupied by research, or what had been his work at
the university, followed immediately by women and music. The

racial laws of '38 had been his first serious *accident along the way* whose only achievement was to make him "political" and hostile to the drafters and promoters of the Racial Manifesto, and particularly toward those cowards who had profited from it to move ahead in their university careers. Toward everyone who had stripped him of his rights from one day to the next and thrown him into the garbage dump of the world for no other reason than the name he carried and that belonged to his ancestors who for centuries had read the Torah and faithfully practiced a different religion. They had believed in a God who did not teach them to fight in order to affirm the superiority of their faith. A religion, in contrast to others, that had never engaged in proselytism, dedicating itself solely to the betterment of mankind.

But that morning he couldn't bring himself to turn his back and walk away. He knew that women and children were closed up inside the Hôtel Bompard, mostly German and Eastern European Jews, and something like a sense of belonging held him there on the sidewalk. He remembered that it was Monday; Monday and Saturday were the days that the police liked to carry out their "public order" operations, so instead of slipping away he moved in closer and closer. He walked right into the middle of the confusion of orders shouted back and forth, bundles and bags piled on top of each other, battered old suitcases with names hastily scribbled on them in chalk, frightened children with ragged jerseys and broken shoes grabbing on to their mothers' skirts. The smell of gasoline and sweat, the police shoving the women onto the trucks and the women, uncertain of their destination, desperately clutching onto overcoats and unrecognizable wool garments, their movements impeded by the children clinging to their bodies. He moved in closer and closer and peremptorily pushed aside the policeman who tried to stop him.

Since he'd arrived in Marseilles he had been living with a young French woman whose husband had gone to England with de Gaulle.

A husband who had more or less his same measurements and whose double-breasted suits he donned with ease. It was that jacket, those beige linen pants styled by a tailor in Paris, that gave him all that self-assurance; and the policeman walked off grumbling something under his breath. In that same instant he realized he had been "sighted." A pair of eyes pierced through the jumble of uniforms and orders flying all around, of pallid faces and hair, the suitcases in a heap in the gray dust of the sidewalk, all of that suffering bunched up outside the door of the hotel. That stare had the cold lucidity of a fox, the panic and the cunning, intelligence sharpened by pain. Moving swiftly and almost inattentively, without allowing anyone else to interfere, a woman thrust a six- or seven-year-old boy at him. Then she turned around and started rummaging through the suitcases piled on the ground as if she were trying to take back her possessions, and immediately two policemen were on her. She fought them off and more policemen arrived and beat her, shoving her violently onto the truck. Her hair, her back in her faded cotton dress, her white calves below the hem of her skirt, disappeared among the other hair, backs, cotton dresses and calves, supported more or less unstably by their tattered shoes. Now the little boy was Arturo's. He took him by the hand and, though he didn't quite know how, suddenly found himself surrounded by the people who were beginning to fill up the Canebière.

With the ragged unkempt boy by the hand he walked right past the two police officers on guard at the end of the street, and squeezing tighter, forced those bare legs to accelerate. Then he mixed in again with the crowd stepping up and down on and off the sidewalks, the bicycles and the screeching trams, the hot sun more and more unbearable. He kept hold of that hand moist with fear, without stopping, and they made their way on foot to Rue de la République.

He and Marie kept the boy with them for a few days, not knowing what to do with him. He gave up his place in the bed and the

123

boy slept with her. Marie washed him down like a little colt and the lice ran down along his bony ribs together with a dark powder. And only when she washed his armpits did he start to giggle, trying to get away from her hand. Marie bought him a white T-shirt and a new pair of shorts.

A quiet boy who sat in the kitchen with his feet on the rung of the chair coloring the pictures in the old fashion magazines that were there in the house. Because of that boy they entered into contact with Les Eclaireurs Israélites and the OSE, a Jewish children's aid organization that said it was willing to take the boy into one of its institutions. From them they learned that his mother had been taken to Les Milles and then transferred to Drancy, in occupied France. But now she knew that her boy was safe. Then he and Marie decided to ask for assistance from HYCEM, an international organization that was less vulnerable at the time, and through HYCEM the boy was placed with a family in the country just outside of Aix-en-Provence. Keeping him in Marseilles could have been dangerous. They promised to take care of the monthly payments to the host family. And when they went to visit him a week later the boy was playing with the ducks and baby chicks. He had gained weight and seemed happy to see them, but then he didn't say anything during the whole visit, sitting with his feet on the rung on the chair as if he were back in the kitchen in Rue de la République. They went back to see him several times, until November, when the British and Americans landed in Algeria and the German troops moved in to occupy the *free zone of Vichy*.

In a matter of days all the rules were turned on their head. All those *papiers* and certificates that had been so hard to get were now worthless, those torn and tattered papers that had stuffed his pockets for all those months; and maybe his name was already on the deportation list. In Rue Paradis, the same shiny villa on the hill where the headquarters of HYCEM had been was now under the command of the Höherer SS und Polizei Führer Oberg and by now

124

even the Red Cross was powerless against the police organized by Darquier de Pellepoix.

But in the meantime he had understood that it was possible to help the others; indeed, one suffered less. There is a fascinating mystery in courage, he tried later to explain to Margot, especially when it works to help others. A power of the will that comes from within and could lead one to believe in the existence of the soul, something that pushes one to look for the light and escape the darkness. The darkness, the shadows, on the contrary, are felt as paralyzing and therefore dangerous.

They tried to get by as best they could until the Gestapo and Touvier's militia started stopping people outside the Gare d'Arenc who were considered vagrants or prostitutes. But above all anyone whose identity card was stamped *Juif*. "Operation Sultan," they called it, for some inexplicable reason of theirs, and over ten thousand police had been brought in from Lyon and Vichy to carry it out. But the real *rafle* began during the night of 23 January, between Friday night and Saturday morning, when it was easier to find families gathered together to celebrate the Sabbath. In a matter of minutes the entire quarter of Vieux-Port was cordoned off as the provident Gestapo forced their way into houses with the help of blacksmiths hired in advance, necessary to break down the doors of those who tried to save themselves by pretending not to be at home.

In an instant Rue Sénac, Rue de l'Académie, Rue Pisançon, and then one by one all of the streets inhabited mostly by Jews echoed with the shattering sound of the boots of the Greiser Division, followed immediately by yelling and the battering down of doors. The women were carried off without even having the chance to get dressed, the sick pulled out of their beds. The screams of mothers rang out, forced to abandon their children (Polizie Führer Oberg would see to them later), and the cries of old people being thrown down the stairs. The rumble of engines and orders yelled up and down the street as the huge eyes of the spotlights reverberated milky white against the dark sky heavy with clouds.

Once the trucks were full they headed for the Sûreté as their headlights shone on the shoes left in the middle of the street, on the indistinguishable garments dropped in the confusion, now sopping wet from the rain. The next morning, when she went out to buy bread, Marie learned that the men and women taken away during the night had been herded together on their feet while they waited to be transferred to prisons in the Bomettes. It was still raining and from the window overlooking Rue de la République, Arturo saw people getting on the tram and stepping up to and down from the sidewalk to avoid the barriers blocking the entrance to Vieux-Port without asking too many questions. Everyone ready to pull out their documents and then to continue on in a hurry, barely a brief glance at all those policemen guarding the intersections, water pouring off their umbrellas.

The glass had been turned upside down again, and this time he was trapped like an insect. Arturo stayed shut in the house until dawn on Sunday, when they heard that Marie's old high school teacher was among the women who had been put on the prison vans in the Bomettes to be deported, packed in so tightly they were forced to hold their arms up above their heads. At the Gare d'Arenc the cattle cars were ready on the tracks to receive them, without enough room to sit down; from there their journey began, the first leg and probably not even the worst. With no water, and only a few sandwiches to be divided up among one thousand five hundred people.

As soon as the curfew was over Marie decided to go to the station to take over some hot drinks and Arturo went with her, carrying the bags full of bottles and thermoses. It was a big risk for him but he felt a strange sense of invulnerability, an awareness that went beyond his being or not being a Jew, and that he would never feel again. As though what he was seeing had projected him beyond fear; something so obscene as to supersede dread and indignation.

But when they arrived at the Gare d'Arenc they weren't allowed to go in; behind the uniforms of the SS they could see a huge number of the round berets and light shirts of Touvier's militia, and they could hear the dogs barking. The weather had turned nice again, clear and cold, the men and women had been separated and were waiting in lines to get on the cattle cars that had been spread with dirty straw; and anyone who hesitated or had difficulty getting on got pushed ahead with a rifle butt. Marie tried to find her elderly former teacher and passing herself off as a nurse she made her way through the militia men and the SS, the railroad workers shocked and dismayed. She was able to get close to the women's line and started handing out the bottles and thermoses. Until someone pushed her away, knocking her off her feet; but the bags were empty by then and the SS were now strutting up and down the platform, sealing the cars, the big doors rolling thunderously and then slamming shut, one after another.

Later that morning loudspeakers mounted on cars deafened the Vieux-Port, ordering all remaining inhabitants to evacuate the area. They had ten hours; after that time anyone still there would be arrested. And on their way back home Arturo and Marie saw entire families coming out of the Vieux-Port, pulling wagons loaded down with mattresses, pots and pans, radios and sewing machines. Others were pushing along bicycles that had all but disappeared under the weight of their amorphous baggage. The storekeepers standing in their doorways looked on in silence at this migration, some of them, despite the cool day, in shirt sleeves. The trams had been requisitioned and were going up the boulevards loaded with furniture and household goods with the owners all packed in together on the rear platform, cold and humiliated by the public exposure of their most intimate possessions. Those who had no one to put them up were rounded up on the shorefront, and as they waited to be taken to a resettlement camp they sat, all bundled up, on chairs, armchairs and stools set out on the asphalt, looking out to the sea, sparkling cold under the sun.

For another week the police continued stopping people on the street and checking documents, and, at the station, searching people getting on and off trains. Battering down doors looking for anyone who, believing the danger had passed, had returned home. There was a curfew in effect from eight in the evening to six in the morning, but all during the night there was an unceasing racket, a mixture of noises like a blast furnace in a steel mill. But it was just the ongoing nightly roundups, interrupted now and again by a gunshot. Until, on the first of February, just after the cathedral bells had played the Angelus, there came a huge explosion that threatened to shatter the window panes in the apartment on Rue de la République. The booming explosions went on for weeks, until the last remaining building in the Vieux-Port had collapsed and the sulfurous cloud that had been hovering darkly in the sky began slowly to disperse, making it possible again to see the azure blue sea. Operation "Sultan" was over and Polizei Führer Oberg could now look down with satisfaction from the height of Rue Paradis upon the work of his explosives experts. Marseilles had been cleansed of its thieves and prostitutes. And above all of its Jews.

Luckily the little boy was safe; and in order to stay close to him Marie moved to Aix-en-Provence while Arturo, with a fake *Ausweis*, fake identity card, and fake food ration cards, managed to make it to the zone occupied by the Italian army. She sent Arturo a postcard, which the boy signed for the first time with his new name: Alain.

In Nice, Arturo continued in his capacity as a "researcher in marine phytoculture." A discipline that did not exist and an office address that corresponded to the concierge's room in a seafront

128

building for blind war veterans. And for the remaining months of the Italian occupation of the French Riviera, all he did was make fake permits for people traveling on trains and on the roads. To enable them to get through the sharp-eyed, meticulous checks of the Gestapo, the scent of their dogs. To help them escape from the undercover spies among the passengers in the train compartments so they could get safely to Mégève, Saint-Martin-de-Vésubie, Valdebor, Saint-Gervais, Thèniers, Sospel.

The mastermind of the whole operation was Angelo Donati, who in the twenties had been among the founders of the Franco-Italian Bank in Paris and had gone on to a successful career in finance. Right up to the day he settled in Nice and made the rescue of Jews the main objective of his life and his money. When they weren't helping him directly the Italian authorities let him go on with his work undisturbed, and Donati had become the reference point for all those groups—Catholic, Protestant, American-Jewish associations and various aid organizations—that were attempting to save as many people as possible from the Endlösung.

Arturo never met him. Donati was one of those characters who strike the imagination of the persecuted because they represent the inversion of the rules that have assigned them their role as victims. He moved about constantly but the Gestapo never managed to get their hands on him, not even when they found out that he was about to obtain a ship to transfer Jews from the French Riviera to Palestine. And on the day word started going around that von Ribbentrop was pressuring Mussolini to arrest him, the officer in charge of Italo-German relations in the Foreign Ministry, Vidau, compiled information he had received from Donati and sent to Mussolini's office in Palazzo Venezia a detailed file on what was happening to Jews in the countries of Eastern Europe.

Arturo's stay in Nice lasted seven months in which he thought of nothing else except how to make his *biffes* as authentic-looking as possible. Of how to get them to their destination sewn inside jacket linings or shoulder pads, rolled up inside the soles of orthopedic shoes. Hidden among the notebooks and the pencil cases inside school bookbags. Seven months during which he turned himself into an expert in the art of forgery, alternating between satisfaction and anxiety. After a day spent as a medieval miniaturist using solvents and inks to create from nothing a non-existent Mademoiselle Bonnard or a Monsieur Lisier, whose namesake lived quietly in Chalon-sur-Saône, he would go sit along the seafront. And then he felt, together with the now familiar sense of insecurity, a new sense of freedom as a supreme good. His gaze drifted out over the sea, mellow and shimmering lightly among the palm trees, and back to the Italian soldiers, the *bersaglieri*, pedaling along with their plumage shining in the sunset, and the old women with their white knit gloves sitting down to eat something that resembled ice cream. The girls walking by arm-in-arm, their imitation silk dresses highlighting every curve of their bodies.

Seven months without a woman; it was the first time it had ever happened to him. Nothing but inventing and falsifying documents, creating "synthetic" Aryans. Enabling them to arrive safe and sound at their destination. Without ever letting his mind wander beyond the limits of those towns: Thèniers, Saint-Martin-de-Vésubie, Sospel, Saint-Gervais, Valdebor. His brain and his hands occupied all day long trying to reconcile photographs and vital statistics of people he'd never seen. Louise Bonnard, black eyes, height 1 meter 64 centimeters, born in Cobourg on 7-5-1923; Pierre Lisier, blue eyes, height 1 meter, 73 centimeters, born in Chalon-sur-Saône on 27-2-1915. . . .

That was his story until 8 September 1943, when once again the bottom fell out like one of those holes dug patiently in the sand that it takes nothing to wipe out, the sides caving in all around instantaneously. Go, go, hurry up and get out of there, the ink still wet on the last *biffes* no longer useful to anyone, the *bersaglieri* in retreat toward Mentone, some on bicycle, some on foot, an occasional car bouncing along in and out of the potholes with bombs on the roof. The only ones left on the seafront are the old women with the white knit gloves, a few curious girls with the wind in their hair as the trucks with the Teutonic cross on the side rumble into view among the palm trees, stinking of low-grade gasoline. Hauptsturmführer Brunner of the Gestapo has arrived and installed himself at number 37bis on the Promenade des Anglais, in what had been up to the day before the beautiful home of Angelo Donati. The Renaults are full of "physiognamists," their eyes squinting under their eyelids to scrutinize the people walking along the street. Every so often the car slows down, behind the window someone raises an index finger to point at a passerby who is more hurried or wary-looking than the others. For every captured Jew the reward is 100 francs.

When an informant's betrayal led to the arrest of Maurice Cachoud, the head of the entire clandestine network of false documents, Arturo and the printer who had worked with him during those seven months went to Chamonix to cross into Switzerland and find safe hiding.

At least that's what they hoped.

All of this was written in the report that was handed over to the secretary of Délivrance; the report that Margot helped compile, or rather which she transcribed on a series of numbered pages. Nicely written pages had never been one of Arturo's strengths, better that he dictate and have Margot write it all down, interrupting him now and again to ask for some clarification or to suggest that he summarize, instead of getting lost in too much detail.

Especially in regard to that first attempt to cross over into Switzerland, when Arturo wants her to describe every moment: from the encounter with the parish priest in Chedde right up to the Diosaz that he was forced to go back up again with the freezing current knifing through his legs while his feet, numb with cold, banged up against the rocks and were left cut and bleeding.

They had started out with eight, plus the guide. The group included a little boy and a teenage girl and to make their way up the Diosaz they formed a chain with them in the middle. But their hands weren't able to hold on to the rope and they kept sliding off, the water drenching their clothes. And when they reached the foot of Buet which rose up to 3,000 meters, the girl went limp and fell to the ground. She was shaking with fever. She had left Warsaw in '39 just in time, and after the Germans occupied Paris she and her brother managed to escape again, this time to the area of southern France occupied by the Italians. But now there was no way to get her back on her feet in that little clearing where she had collapsed, as if her body had dissolved into the grass, her clothes and cloth shoes soaked and frozen. The guide protested, they couldn't stop there, they'd be risking everybody's lives. But the girl was all curled up on the ground with tears streaming down like water, and so in the end they were forced to leave her there together with her brother. After Buet they still had to climb up and down the other side of Cheval Blanc and the guide didn't let them rest until late in the afternoon, for half an hour in a ravine surrounded by huge rocks with the wind blowing ice cold against their backs. Then they went back to climbing up the Col de Vieux, and when they got to the top and could look down at the blue patch of Lake Barberine inside Swiss territory, the guide left them. It took them another two hours before they saw the little stone house at the border station: it appeared to them in the night like the stable in Bethlehem, the red flag with the white cross barely waving under the stars. A vision that seemed to last a long time but also no more than *le temps d'un soupir* (but how can one write this without getting lost in useless details? Yes, write it, write *le temps d'un soupir*) because almost immediately a rather gruff sergeant declared that only the little boy could stay, all the others had to be sent back. . . .

132

The little boy started sobbing, his arms wrapped around his head. When they'd started out his father had declared his age as twelve but he was certainly younger than that and he had borne up under the fatigue and the fear the whole way there without ever complaining. Now nobody was able to calm him down, his bare swollen feet hanging down purple from the chair next to the wood stove. Later on a soldier brought him some milk and hot soup and the boy immediately fell asleep, his face dirty with mud and tears, sunk down in the straw. He looked dead. Around four in the morning the sergeant came around again to say he had managed to obtain a pass for the boy's father too, but for the others there was nothing he could do, in a few hours he would accompany them back to the French border at Col de Vieux.

But being taken back to the border meant ending up in the maw of Hauptsturmführer Brunner; and as soon as the sergeant had gone away, he and the printer had escaped, taking advantage of the little bit of moonlight that was rising up from the mountains. And only the animal strength that comes from the desire to survive enabled them to search for the tracks they'd left in the snow on Cheval Blanc and then again on Mt. Buet, the long scrape marks on the rock. Their feet wounded and torn and their backs bent under the weight of their packs. They lost their way several times and risked ending up on the bottom of a gorge, but they finally made their way back to the clearing where they'd left the Polish girl (*the grass was still trampled down and there was the wrapping from a box of biscuits, the bottle that had held the cognac, empty, write it down, write it down*). And it wasn't until the evening of the next day that they were able to get back to Chedde where the same parish priest who had helped them before treated the wounds on their feet and tried to alleviate the ones in their souls. Assuming there is such a thing as a soul.

Pages and pages, read and reread, corrected together and then placed by Margot in a large orange envelope whose glued edges she licked all around. Arturo shoved it into his pocket; she told him no, that way it'll get wrinkled, and gave him a folder with cloth corners. And the next day Arturo walked all over town before he was able to find Place Palud and then he had to wait two hours in the waiting room at Délivrance before he could hand over the envelope to an amiable woman with a formal smile; and as he watched her place it on top of a pile of other envelopes he realized how that experience that had seemed so dramatic to him could actually appear insignificant compared to others. So many; too many, and some that ended in death or torture at the hands of the Gestapo.

But at least Margot, if she loved him as much as she said, with all that she had been writing down, at least she should have made it her own. Accepted it not only with her head but like a liquid that goes right to your gut; and afterward you are different, you don't know how, you don't know how much. Different, and you hope better. But she is tired, she's sleepy, it seems to her she's demonstrated her love enough by writing and correcting and then going back to write again, a continuous flow of pages that Arturo kept scribbling on because he wanted to keep adding more and more details. She feels she demonstrates her love every day, standing at the glistening, storied cash register wearing her black satin smock. On Sundays when it rains sometimes they go to the Capitol Cinema, but if the weather is nice they go across town to the lake to sit on the shore. Scared by their arrival, some ducks wobble away across the lawn to dive back into the water. She always keeps looking around afraid she'll recognize some friend of Mamigna's among those matrons walking by in their hats, their dogs on leashes. Then she pulls out the sweets that Mademoiselle Janton has given her for Sunday and she always lets Arturo eat more of them, happy to see them disappear instantly into his mouth. A mouth she never tires of looking at as he goes through one after another of the colorful *petits fours*, the puff-pastry *palmiers*, the crumbs on his thin dry lips. A mouth that sometimes upsets her for its capacity to express a sudden, disconcerting sadness.

But then neither should Arturo have forgotten her willingness in putting on that black smock every morning, smiling at him reflected in the mirror on the dresser as she fastened that mortifying boarding-school-girl collar. And when the days started getting longer and Mademoiselle Janton kept up her insipid unchanging chatter, her thoughts couldn't help but turn to Vivia and Marisetta, to Eddy. To their *fantastic* returns to Chesa Silvascina with the snow melting under their boots and the great expanse of the lake deserted. No one dares go venture out on it anymore, the first livid patches of water making their way through the ice and snow as the air stings their cheeks and the sun disappears, filling the sky with every possible shade of yellow. And Arturo should have remembered their first room in Coira, where there was no way even to turn around, and every time she needed to find a pair of stockings she had to turn the entire suitcase inside out, that cat smell wafting up out of the dust-filled corners. The evening visits of Doctor Zurhaus sitting there listening to music in silence, his eyes closed and his hands folded on his vest, while she gave it everything she had to be happy. He should have remembered these and a lot of other things in that anonymous and pleasant city in Rhode Island when the brutal truth about their baby boy had acted as a solvent and precipitated the rose-tinted powder that until that moment had colored their life together. And made them see it for what it was. Sand, nothing but sand, and tinged with suspicious dark stains.

3

For a long time Margot continued to think of Eddy with remorse and anger. Remorse for having somehow betrayed him, failing to take his feelings into account; anger because he had behaved in such a despicable manner.

She had been tempted to talk with Arturo various times about what happened on that afternoon in the room with the yellow chaise. But during all of those months it wasn't possible even to bring up the subject. She knew that as far as Arturo was concerned there was no possible justification; and while at first he had judged Eddy as foolish and presumptuous, when he found him in his room rummaging through his drawers he had branded him a traitor.

She wanted to explain to him how much Eddy had suffered from being ostracized by Mamigna, the problems created by his clumsy, hulking body; he who was the son of a man who was so handsome and charming. How she, Margot, had been such an important part of his life, and how jealousy must have made him furious. But every time she tried her mind went into a fog, the sentences she spoke so vague and unfocused that they lost all meaning. Something in Arturo stopped her from going on; he would never show any forgiveness or understanding for those who informed on Jews or even just blackmailed them. The flames are starting to eat away at your clothes, he said one time, and they come and throw a can of gasoline on you. . . .

One night in bed, while they were talking about his arrival at Chesa Silvascina, she was reminded of that strange lingo Eddy used to speak with Vivia and Marisetta so no one else would be able to understand them, a mixture of Italian and German. "Eddy was the one who invented it," she said, "he is really good at that kind of thing." "Someday we'll talk about Eddy," he cut her off, "but not now, I can't now, I don't want to talk about him. Not for any reason at all." She felt offended by such a peremptory refusal and tried to respond. Too much bitterness, too much, she thought, and she said the word Forgiveness. In the end, she said, forgiving makes us better. But Arturo switched off the light and in the darkness his voice sounded strangely weak: "*Never, please, never.*"

And in May '45, when Margot went back to Geneva for the first time to see Mamigna, she burst into tears when she heard the news of Eddy's death. They were sitting at a café on the thin strip of land between the Rhone and Lake Geneva and suddenly she felt as if she were blind, the tears streaming down into her mouth. The anger and remorse that for the past year had gradually been fading and blending together were now brought back violently to the surface by death. The tenderness she had felt for Eddy seemed to wash over her in waves and make her feel pity for him and for herself. She hadn't been able to save him; on the contrary she had turned against him. Not even for a moment did she doubt the theory that it had been an accident. And when Signora Arnitz mentioned the photographs they'd found in his pockets, she imagined they were the pictures of her that Eddy always carried with him. "Of you? That's extremely unlikely," Signora Arnitz said, "we found the pictures of you in pieces in the waste basket in his room. You girls are too narcissistic, you always think the world revolves around you." Her irritation made her turn away from her daughter to look at a swan plunging its head into the water to snatch a piece of bread being pulled downstream by the current. And when she turned back to look at Margot, she found her absorbed as if she were contemplating some interior image of herself and Eddy. "It appears that the tragedy," Signora Arnitz added cuttingly, "wasn't so much a matter of chance as an assisted accident." But again it was as if Margot had felt herself being accused for what had been a kind of dizzy spell, not to say a state of desperation; and she shivered as she blew her nose, despite the mild May air.

The Russians had entered Berlin and the Thousand-Year Reich was now an endless field of ruins. All of Europe was pulling out its flags and the wine hidden in the basement to celebrate in the streets. In Geneva too, as if a gigantic bag of confetti had been emptied out on the streets, diplomats and refugees thronged together with servants, spies, and soldiers. They sat on the benches along the edges of the lawns, walked across the bridges, drank together at tables in the sun. Margot seemed ready to take back possession of her colorful spring suits and the tennis skirts that highlighted her slim suntanned legs. The shoes still there waiting for her, veiled by a thin layer of dust. Signora Arnitz looked at her with her piercing blue eyes. Those months in Geneva had rejuvenated her and her cheeks were shiny and full, her hair just a bit grayer tucked under a light blue cloth hat, held firm by a pin; and in the shade of the hat her hurriedly painted lips opened to ask her favorite daughter to leave the man with whom she had gone away from Chesa Silvascina. "If that's the reason you wanted to see me," she answered, "it would have been better not to meet." Then Signora Arnitz tried to re-open the discussion of the accident theory. Her suspicion and Marisetta's, she said, was that someone had assisted that fall into the Inn. But Margot stood up, indignant. "What are you saying?" her voice choking off inside her throat and Signora Arnitz grabbed her arm to force her to sit down again. "If that's what you thought, why didn't you go to the police?" Margot's heart pounded against her chest with rage. And Signora Arnitz changed the subject. But by now it was open war between them, and perhaps more from anger than from a desire to triumph over what she felt was the silly and arrogant naiveté of a little girl, Signora Arnitz decided to play the trump card of money. She did it brutally, threw it down on the table between the coffee pitcher and the sugar, the tablecloth with the fringe around the edges. As long as you remain with that man, she said, *kein Geld*, not even a franc; and her eyebrows furrowed to reinforce the hardness of that *kein Geld*: the time for playing games is over, my dear, for you too the time has come to start distinguishing between "money" and "no money" as her eyes stared at her like two enameled buttons sunk into her face. She certainly knew how risky this approach was with Margot but she was tired of pretending and probably imagined that all those months of doing without had made her daughter more accommodating on the subject. She was wrong; Margot was still the fearless girl who defied the world, and she was also in love (she, who was so expert in such matters, shouldn't have underestimated that). She was standing up again, red in the face, and Signora Arnitz was afraid she was going to make a scene. "I'm going to marry him," she said, "as soon as the papers are ready, that's what I came to tell you. I'm expecting a baby," she dared her, her big chestnut eyes, still wet from her tears for Eddy, illuminated by her refusal. The light blue blouse of any ordinary girl, the badly cut skirt. "*Es ist nicht möglich, er ist ein Teufel!*" Signora Arnitz's voice died in her throat, she felt as if she had suddenly been struck dumb. "You can speak Italian, nobody is listening to us. . . ." she was contemptuous, she was feeling strong despite her pain for Eddy, a pain full of bile that now seemed to take the form of that woman sitting across from her who thought she could buy her like that hat and that pearl hatpin. "*Ein Teufel*" Signora Arnitz said again, and then she followed her with her eyes as Margot passed between the tables, her shoes catching in the gravel. She watched her push open the iron gate and go outside the café fence and head across the bridge with the wind ruffling her hair. Without looking back even once. Margot started crying again.

The baby was born in November and by the end of January he had already gone, in a sort of big box lined with white satin, when the icy streets of Providence emptied again after the chatter and the racing around that had animated them during the Christmas holidays and the early darkening days painted frost-covered branches that broke at the slightest touch. But Margot didn't leave Rhode Island until June.

In the beginning (the early days, *after*) Arturo had gotten into the habit of coming home late in the evening and she would hear him going from one room to another, opening and closing the refrigerator. Furiously splitting the wood for the fireplace. In Providence for the first time they felt like they were almost rich, with no problems if they wanted to go out to dinner one night or if she needed a new overcoat. When they first arrived they spent a lot of money for the baby, too, for the crib and the colored wallpaper. They even bought an electric heater so it would be warmer when they gave him a bath. And now they had enough coal in the basement to run the furnace for months; there was no need to light the fireplace. But anyway Arturo would fool around for half-hours at a time with the paper and the little bundles of kindling wood, delicately blowing on the fire so it would rise up to lick the bigger logs. Then he would sit there doing nothing and just watch it, his feet up on the table and the cigarettes burning one after another. He was waiting, that's how it was at the beginning.

If she had been different, less secure and not so brash, and if above all she had been able to see her own story as one of many among the millions of painful stories. If she hadn't thought of love as a precious flower reserved especially for her, to cultivate in her own private garden, then maybe they would have long since been able to work out a solution together for what had happened. But Margot wasn't even able to imagine *that truth*; she was too young, too "spoiled," Arturo said once, accustomed to viewing people and events in relation to herself and her way of judging them. Even her generosity was part of this way of looking at the world. And the thing that she called *feeling* was pushed higher and higher by physical attraction. Arturo seemed to her to correspond in every way to what her body felt was desirable; and just like the current fed by the wind on the lake, her desire quickly expanded from one shore to the other, filling up all the space. From that moment on nothing was the same as before or even interesting outside of the magic circle drawn around the presence of Arturo. Away from him, all light became dim. That's the way it was at Chesa Silvascina; and then later on in Coira and in Fribourg, in Trieste. Up until the baby was born.

When the time *to know* had finally come. When from one day to the next what was left of the self-assured, attractive girl who went to greet Arturo for the first time in the entryway at Chesa Silvascina had to recognize her defeat. Accept an enormous truth, a reality that was beyond all the imaginable possibilities. And for one of those strange coincidences of life, Time, that damned measure of *before* and *after*, placed the moment for discovering the truth immediately *after* the death of the baby. Even though by then that truth and the death of the baby were separated by an interval of years.

A baby who had seemingly come apart, slowly, piece by piece, his mouth finally without breath altogether. Beautiful and to all appearances perfect, a baby that was supposed to reconcile her features with Arturo's and become the tangible proof of their adventurous story of escape and salvation; and instead he had been transformed into a bundle to be thrown into the pile along with all those innocents who had suffered so atrociously and undergone the most wicked injustices.

The room in Providence had wallpaper with little yellow roses, ruffled nylon bedspreads and a ridiculous Chinese pagoda lamp. That was the first thing they would have replaced if they had stayed in that house rented with one month's rent in advance in preparation for the baby. Now she was staring obsessively at that lamp as if it were the source of all their misfortune. "He never would have done it," she said; she was shaking and the words struggled to get out of her mouth as dry as if a blotter had soaked up all her saliva;

"he never would have done it," the name Eddy that had been a pang in her heart now sounded sweet and putrid. "But you know damn well he was on his way to inform on me. You were the first one to say so that afternoon." "That's not true, I was just afraid that he might lose his head in a moment of rage, that's why I wanted you to go after him, to explain to him. . . ." She squeezed herself down into the couch as if she could find shelter there from the image that obsessed her; her face pressed against the upholstery that still seemed to be imbued with the slightly rancid smell of the baby's milk. "But he never would have informed on you, I don't believe that, I'll never believe that, I knew him, you didn't—" "Then why did he go rummaging through my drawers? Why was he holding my passport in his hand? He'd even copied down my vital statistics, he had them on a piece of paper in his pocket—" "So then the reason you went after him was to kill him . . . that was the only thing you had in mind, all you were thinking about was saving yourself." "Ah, the monstrous logic of women that distorts every argument to turn it to their favor . . . Certainly I was thinking of saving myself, so I wouldn't have to go back to being a mouse trying to scamper away from the broom." "You knew I would have protected you anywhere and no matter what, at the cost of my life." "I wouldn't be so sure about that if I were you. . . . Anyway, I've always preferred to take care of myself, I've got the right to, just like everybody else. Or maybe you think that's not so, that being a Jew is itself some kind of stigma, a fault? That's what you think, that in any case I was destined to be a victim. Then you might even have tried to save me . . . Is that your idea of justice?" She didn't respond, her eyes staring at those little yellow roses climbing up the wall like a procession of frogs. Arturo grabbed her by the arms, trying to force her to look him in the eye. The double-hung window was open a crack and the yellow curtain was fluttering in the air behind him. "Margot, I would do it again, listen to me, I was forced to do it, I would be again in the same circumstances, he was there waiting

143

for the coach to go turn me in. The first person to pay would have been Doctor Zurhaus. Haven't you ever thought of that?" But now it was as if that dead baby were Eddy and Margot's body rebelled. She didn't want that pang in her heart, she didn't want to see anything anymore; never again that face she had so often kissed and caressed, never again the houses in Providence and the trees with the squirrels, never again to see those curtains billowing in the breeze or hear the sharp sound of the sliding sash that stopped the horrible fluttering of the yellow rayon. "I'm Catholic," she said suddenly, "I can't understand."

Afterward they tried again to talk about it, sitting in the living room that opened onto the yard of birch trees. Or in their room, lying on the bed, while the silence that had occupied the house after the baby's death stretched out its tentacles in the dark. But they never made love again; it seemed like so long since the last time, a few days before the baby was born. That night they lay there beside each other, as if their bodies were incapable of separating and all of a sudden something moved inside her, almost as though waves were moving deeply through her lower body. Waves formed by those elbows, those knees, those feet just a few centimeters long, and they laughed together in the dark.

Now they were uncomfortable in the darkness of their room. In order to talk they had to turn on the light and the Chinese pagoda lampshade shook its red tassels, it even seemed there was sound coming from its little brass pendants. In that light they looked into each other's eyes to try to understand, or at times to challenge one another or encourage each other to keep on talking. But it didn't help much. At other times their gaze came to rest on the objects in the room, as if to impress upon their torment the stamp of dull, daily routine.

The baby's tragic death should have brought them together; so she thought at first. But almost immediately that worm started working in her brain; she would wake up suddenly in the night as if Mamigna were standing over her with those finely honed azure eyes in the shadow of her hat: *my suspicion and Marisetta's is that someone assisted that fall . . .* the cube of sugar plopping into the cup, the two of them almost floating with the table and the tablecloth in the current of the Rhone. *You girls are too narcissistic, you always think the world revolves around you. . . .* The lips that opened and closed on the words were not as full as they once had been and the lipstick was spreading, oozing into the tiny, invisible wrinkles. Mamigna, she knows so well, doesn't like to lie for the sake of lying, on the contrary she prefers the cruel use of the truth. *Pictures of you? We found them in pieces in the waste basket in his room. . . .* The words reverberate through the darkness in the room in Providence, ricocheting from one corner to the next in search of an answer different from the one growing in her brain like a tumor. And after he had reduced them to pieces (with scissors, with his hands, ripping them apart?), WHAT HAPPENED NEXT?

When Eddy went outside, closing the door quietly so he wouldn't be heard, she saw him from the window, his shoulders bulging in his fur jacket, hatless under the falling snow. He walked fast, putting on his wool gloves. Cold hands had always been a problem for him; even when he went skiing he always had to take an extra pair of gloves in case he lost them. She looked at her watch and remembered that the postal coach for Silvaplana would be coming soon. Then she ran downstairs, she wanted to stop him before he reached the square. But then in the vestibule she stopped herself, her hands still dirty with the blood she'd wiped from his face.

Questions that keep revolving around the same thought, getting tighter and tighter with every revolution, the margin getting smaller and smaller, that dead baby weighing on her mind like Christ on the shoulders of Saint Christopher. *They found him at the opening into Lake Champfèr, he must have been there for months, he was almost naked . . .* the smell of Mamigna's face powder, the little pitcher of milk. *So it happened at Silvaplana*, Margot says, Lake Champfèr is just below there. *That's not certain at all, the current could have dragged him along for kilometers.* . . . Mamigna has that string of pearls and turquoise around her neck that she used to give her to play with when she was a little girl sick in bed. But then, as soon as she was well again, she took it back. *Le collier-jeu* they called it. *It appears that the tragedy wasn't so much a matter of chance as an assisted accident.* . . . But the coach driver knew Eddy very well, he must remember whether he got on the coach that evening, at that hour the coach is almost always empty. *He probably died of suffocation.* . . . The gloves, she should have asked her, did anyone find his gloves under the snow at Champfèr? Instead she said: *I'm expecting a baby*. Somebody was throwing some bread down from the bridge, the swan's head dived to fish it out, forming a white arch of feathers. Mamigna was moving her hand up to her neck as if someone had wounded her, sticking the knife in there, *Es ist nicht möglich, er ist ein Teufel* . . . the black eye of the swan swimming away. Then from up on the bridge, through the quivering tears, she saw the teal, the widgeons, and the garganeys rising up from the water in groups, batting their wings. *Ein Teufel* . . .

"My only fault," Arturo said, "is that I let you believe that Eddy disappeared into the night like an elf in the mountains." He had accepted the compromise with what she wanted to think and that kept him safe from any negative reaction. The truth needs force to affirm itself, and in that moment he was very weak from the enormous effort it had cost him to kill a man. A coward, a miserable wretch ready to sell him because of a stupid desire for revenge.

But Margot cannot accept *that* truth. And her refusal turns into something physical that has to do with her shaken body, gone to pieces together with that baby with the bobbing head who was no longer able to breathe, his gasping becoming softer and softer like the crinkling of tissue paper. How can Arturo ask so much of her now? Not only must she come to know that truth, watch it circumscribe itself with the precise outline of a drawing on a sheet of paper, but she should also be willing to share it in the name of justice. Or of love? No, love has nothing to do with it. . . .

And in the face of her horror Arturo grew more rigid. The horror belongs to Eddy, he said, it involves all those like him, the jackals that inhabited Europe. It is a question of justice and instead she was turning it into a question of pity.

But Margot closed herself up like a hedgehog around a single argument: *Eddy would never have done it.* Obtuse and stubborn, crouched up on the worn-out springs of the couch, she shook her head. And now the baby's death lost all chance of relief and took on a ghostlike face of biblical dimensions. It was the finger of God pointing at them. "Why do you think he went out into all that snow? Do you want me to describe the shock on his face when I caught up with him? Do you want to listen to me all the way to the end, at least one time?" "I don't want to hear about it." She covered her ears so she couldn't hear him and saw Arturo's lips moving and him suffering and the more she saw him suffer the more she thought that that was justice, that he should suffer. It didn't even matter to her anymore that he should bow to his pain, ask her forgiveness for the wrong he had been forced to do to her. She no longer wanted anything.

"And then you lied to me." "Lied is not the right word." To control himself Arturo is pacing back and forth, a cigarette between his fingers and his unbuttoned jacket hanging down around his hips. His legs long and thin, the irregular face with the dimpled jaw and the high cheek bones. She likes looking at him, continues to be attracted by him to a degree that's almost shameful, but that only makes her more obstinate in her bill of indictment. "Isn't it the same thing, to let someone believe something that is the opposite of the truth? Isn't that lying?" "Okay, so I lied to you." He's stopped pacing, the sound of his footsteps has stopped, Arturo is standing in

147

front of her waiting for some gesture, some kind of a sign, maybe just an expression of doubt in place of that terrible certainty of which she's convinced she's an emissary. But she doesn't budge, it's as if she's plastered to that orange-striped couch, she still wants him but that's a fault and she won't let herself so much as touch his hand. "I wasn't brave enough. I was afraid," he said again. "Afraid he would turn you in?" she asked? "No, I was never afraid of that. Afraid that you would leave me. I never would have made it alone." "You still had Doctor Zurhaus." "But I needed you." He bends down to pick up a piece of the newspaper that had slipped onto the floor, folds it up and puts it away. She looks at his hands, strong and dark. The hands that killed Eddy, the same hands that she still wants, in such a foolishly absurd way, to feel on her body. "And later, after we were free?" "Afterward, it was even harder, we came here, you were happy . . . I kept thinking that someday I would be able to tell you." "When?" "I don't want to talk about it. It doesn't matter. One day, and you would understand." "What? That it's possible to kill someone without pity?" "Pity has nothing to do with it!"

Margot looked away from him, suddenly exhausted. "But did you really love me, or did it just make you feel good to think you did? Or was it simply convenient?" she blurted out. "I refuse to respond to that; it's vulgar."

"A silly woman" he said once about the wife of the head of the biology department who was always talking about the beauty of nature. "A silly woman." She turned away so she wouldn't have to bear up under his gaze. Outside a pale white sun had appeared and it was shining annoyingly on the glass table top, on the cup still half full of coffee. A watery, dark liquid, ice cold by now. She drank it down slowly. She felt homesick for Trieste and for their room that looked out on the sea. She felt that if they could just go back there the spell would be broken. Happiness was trapped back there between the curtains and the smell of the sea, the big creaking bed where they always ended up in the crack in the middle between the two old mattresses. "Your justice cannot be my justice," she said suddenly, "I don't want your justice, it's repugnant."

She was curled up on the couch; perhaps the Polish girl had curled up like that on the meadow at the foot of Buet. Who knows what became of her? Back in Chedde no one had seen them again, neither her nor her brother. Arturo's voice came to her muffled now by the back of the couch. "I was supposed to accept being a victim," he was saying, "after all, a lot of people accepted it, that wouldn't have been repugnant for you, it's nice to devote oneself to victims, it's noble. . . ." "It's still better than being on the other side, on the side that kills," she answered, her mouth pressed against the back of the couch. "But what do you know about the victims? I've seen them, the victims . . ." She closed her eyes, now it was dark. "And you're not even a real Jew, you're not even circumcised" her breath coming back to her warm off the upholstery. She didn't know why she'd said it. Maybe now he would slap her and she would be able to scream. Scream Eddy's name and her own. Eddy and Margot, Eddy and Margot, Eddy and Margot . . . But Arturo remained silent; slowly the pain loosened its grip, became confused, became the day, the light on the glass table top, the buzz of the refrigerator. Those eyes that were staring at her, suddenly distant and absent as if they were struggling to distinguish her curled up against the back of the couch.

4

At the beginning she was just looking for a couple of rooms where she could put some of the furniture that was left after the sale of Chesa Silvascina, mostly things that nobody else wanted and that had been left piled up in the garage. And it wasn't that she'd been thunderstruck by the place; as a girl she'd passed by there a few times on day trips to Davos through the Flüelapass. In those days there was a spring where they stopped to fill their canteens. But then, a little bit at a time, while visiting other houses in other valleys, she started thinking again about that sort of a ruin she had seen at the beginning. Because it wasn't anything more than a ruin; and in the end she realized that that was "the place." She wasn't the one who made the choice but the one who was chosen; "someone" or "something" had made the decision for her. There were moments when she almost felt the weight of a choice that she had been forced to accept. Something like what must have happened in the past to European settlers when they arrived in the wide-open spaces of America. Mamigna had given her the money. Despite everything, Mamigna wanted her to be *well fed and well housed*.

A lot of things changed right away: her notion of cold and hot. The meaning of sounds. But what changed most of all was her relationship with words. Some buried themselves underground, others that had been muted or invisible for years reawakened to the point of urgency. Even solitude was different. Now it had a clearly defined horizon, a weight that was light on some days and dense and painfully heavy on others. Little openings from which to look out at the world as from inside the visored helmet that imprisoned the face of medieval knights.

Arturo lived together with Marie for a few years and then they got married. She didn't oppose the divorce; it didn't even make her feel bad. It all seemed suddenly very distant, and without her even making a conscious choice, men disappeared from her life. Men understood in the frontal sense, the men one wants to please. The ones we'd like to count in our lives, for better or worse.

It wasn't a sacrifice, it came to her naturally like so many other things since she'd decided to settle down there. Already in the first winter (the same one in which Arturo remarried) she realized that that was a place where there was no room for certain types of relationships. No room even in the physical sense. Freedom had been transformed into a good to be enjoyed in the wild, something that could easily be contaminated. She sometimes felt like one of those animals that copulate only far away from their dens, and only at certain times of the year. *A grouse, a fox*, she said. And then a short raucous laugh seemed to take the meaning out of everything she had just said.

She had a way of laughing, letting her head fall back (the way Isabella too used to laugh once) that always took Lorenza by surprise. Even her sense of humor, which distorted her face into an oddly childlike grin, always came as a surprise. It was as if a part of her had regressed to a time somewhere between infancy and adolescence, when one's reactions no longer belong to the former but not yet to the latter, suspended in a kind of metaphysical ether. Something that was capable of manifesting itself without warning if someone, having intuited that they were dealing with a woman who was different from the farm woman she appeared to be, started asking questions. Then she would give the most astonishing answers, her disarmingly naïve smile curling the skin around her eyes into hundreds of tiny wrinkles. And others, with the excuse of wanting to see her pillows, would go inside and look around the rooms, expressing their amazement at the originality of the fabrics and the inlaid furniture that she had dug up in some of the old mountain shelters. Then she would start talking to herself in dialect, closing the doors with a bang, and refuse to wrap whatever they had bought or even to sell it to them; and just like that her old behavior put her back into a position of command, almost as if she were dealing with servants. But while she wasn't joking she wasn't really serious either. She was just irreverent.

She sang. At night her voice came through the wooden room divider like a radio left on by mistake. Her voice didn't sound like her; moody, varied, hitting the strident notes of songs from the 1940s or rising solemnly as though she were accompanying an organ. Or transforming itself into a limpid, acute falsetto. Her repertory was remarkably varied and followed no apparent logic; it was useless to try to talk about it with her the next day. Set into her wrinkled face, her large chestnut eyes, a color that in the morning sun looked like burnt sugar, seemed not to understand the meaning of the questions, serenely occupied with the little world that revolved around her.

But that time that she heard her intone the *Dies irae* Lorenza couldn't resist and opened the door where she was sitting at the loom. Her voice rose deep, coarse, fascinating in the silence of the night; and not until she came to the last stanza, with the brisk beat of the spool like the rhythmic swing of a pendulum, did Margot turn to Lorenza, standing in the doorway in her nightgown: "What do you want?" she asked. She had just finished a pillow and was sitting at the smallest loom, the lamp shining on her dilated, absent-looking eyes. "Sing it one more time," Lorenza asked her. "So you like that funeral pyre music?" she laughed, the dyed woolen threads moving back and forth through her fingers. "Please, just one more time," Lorenza insisted. She looked at her for just a minute as if she were asking herself how she could get rid of this nuisance, then she went back to her work and her breathing swelled the back of her cotton dress. When she was singing she was happy, defenseless. A girl again, and nothing else but a girl; and her voice seemed born of her unsatisfied desires, with nothing religious about it, devouring the verses, crushing them one against the other. But when she came to the end her back seemed to bend in half, spent, her body inert, weighing heavy on the stool, as her voice dragged along through the final stanzas, *Quid sum miser tunc dicturus? Quem patronum rogaturus*— "Enough, go back to bed, it's cold in here," she said, turning around suddenly. She got up and stretched out her arms, opening and closing her small wrinkled hands into fists as children do. And then she started turning out the lights, clearly wishing to be left alone.

But the next day she confessed to Lorenza that what she had sung for her was only the first part of the *Dies irae*; the whole thing was much too long and ended up becoming monotonous, losing all its force. Every once in a while she had to sing it in church and the beginning seemed to have something transporting about it. It was triumphant, liberating, representing the victory of faith over doubt. But if you happen to catch me singing *Star Dust* or one of those songs I used to sing when I was young, she added with that slightly wry look on her face, then you'd better come in a hurry to console me, it means that sadness is wringing my heart. . . .

On the ocean liner that brought her back to Europe in '46 she shared a cabin with a former opera singer. At that special moment the encounter with that woman who had made music her reason to live was the first patch of blue in the otherwise leaden gray sky of her days. For a few hours the torment of "being Margot" disappeared, God picked her up again by her ponytail. And shut in their cabin with a glass of water, even when the others didn't dare get out of their beds for the rolling of the ship, the two of them kept on tirelessly with their trills.

154

With Arturo it was over. That wall that had grown up so quickly between them, a little bit higher with each passing day, suddenly revealed itself to be a vacuum. An absence vaster and more impenetrable than any solid obstacle. Arturo stopped splitting wood and lighting the fire, stopped contemplating the flames as the ashtray filled with cigarette butts. He went back to being kind again, almost ceremonious, and when he went out he worried about her staying home alone and arranged for the wife of one of his colleagues to come stay with her. He even brought her the program of the Manning Chapel choir, which met two times a week. A choir that would be more than happy to have her, he added, if she wanted to become a member.

He started sleeping in the upstairs room, the one that they'd decided when they first moved in would be the guest room. Guests who never came. She heard him getting out of bed in the morning while it was still dark and then starting the car to go to the beach at Moonstone. That's where he would begin his walk along the water still livid with the light of dawn as the seagulls took off and landed again just a short distance away, and then took off again and flew a little farther on as if they were overseeing his walk. And when Margot offered to go with him he seemed happy; but right from that first morning she realized she couldn't keep up with him. She still hadn't regained her full strength, partly because of the breastfeeding that she'd had to interrupt from one day to the next, a series of ups and downs that her system had tolerated less than she'd expected. Arturo stopped to wait up for her but surely if he had been alone he would have walked much farther and enjoyed it more, kilometers of beach whose entire length he would have walked with his long legs, his oilskins bulging in the wind. So after that first morning Margot gave up, and she would hear him coming down the stairs in the dark and moving around cautiously in the kitchen trying not to make noise; then the front door would snap shut and silence filled the room again. She would lie there awake waiting for the first light to slip in under the curtains and spread out on the opposite wall, the long black ribbon of the night quickly giving way to that procession of yellow frogs. Then she would close her eyes again and wait for sleep to return.

Sometimes she dreamt, other times she stayed awake as the birds began to make their racket, calling to each other in the trees. One by one she recognized the sounds announcing the beginning of the day until she got up and made herself breakfast in the kitchen. "Muffins" with maple syrup that she slowly dipped in her coffee with the radio on, looking out at that yard of birch trees; and an enormous desire to let herself go. To throw herself down on the floor, writhing and screaming. The radio was tuned to a station operated by the Coast Guard, and the Marine Corps hymn with its squealing brass and rolling drums accompanied her slow chewing of those sickly sweet muffins. The stream of orange juice flowing down from the electric squeezer. An instrument that could instantly roar and vibrate violently, drowning out the triumphant notes of the military band. Then the impulse to curl up on the floor intensified; to pull out her hair and claw at herself until she was overwhelmed by physical pain. Instead she sipped the juice of those big oranges from Florida and went to open the door for the cleaning lady. And she envied her obesity, her face with the double chin and glasses, the calves marked by varicose veins. Her serene passing from one room to another with the vacuum cleaner. She wanted to be her, Johanna.

Arturo had started going to Zionist meetings in the evenings but his skepticism showed; just for curiosity he said. In the end his gentile mother, to whom he had always been very grateful for his secular upbringing, hadn't been able to erase a sense of belonging that the events of the war had then made much sharper. Not that he felt capable of believing in God, he would say, but to know which God and why and how one believes, that perhaps was important. By now it was part of his life. She, Margot, had made a very meaningful statement that time she said she couldn't understand him because she was Catholic. Or that his idea of justice was horrifying to her.

He began writing to Marie again to ask for news about the little boy. As soon as conditions permitted, Marie had gone to get him again and in her letter she described the great joy of that moment: the boy ran to pack his suitcase and then he grabbed her hand without letting go until they had boarded the train. His mother had died at Auschwitz and there was no further news of his father, who had been taken prisoner by the Germans in Silesia in 1939. Marie had been awarded custody, *un petit garçon remarquable*, and, out of a sense of duty, but also to fulfill her own desire, they had gone back to live in Marseilles, where he now attended Hebrew school. They were back in the apartment in Rue de la République and as she wrote the boy was doing his homework, sitting at the kitchen table the way he used to do back then.

Arturo sent him some blue jeans from Providence together with a T-shirt with the university insignia, and Margot helped him wrap the package.

It was over; day after day she was forced to recognize it. If Arturo had ever loved her, his love had now sunk to the bottom, there was nothing left except those air bubbles that appear on the surface for an instant and then dissolve. It was over for Arturo but not for her. The "transport," what she used to call feeling because she couldn't think of another name for it, was still intense. Mixed and confused with bitterness, it thrashed about like an animal caught in a trap. But it didn't mean anything anymore, it couldn't even be transformed into an instrument of blackmail. That's the way things had gone and that was it. Without any uproar and without a lot of tears. While they talked sitting on the couch with the worn-out springs. While Arturo paced back and forth with the soles of his shoes barely audible on the carpet and the words became glued forever to that yellow wallpaper. Or again under the reddish light of that pagoda-shaped lamp. *Verba volant, scripta manent.* But that wasn't true, words could carry infinitely more weight than any writing because they had the added benefit of the voice and the facial expression, the gestures of the person who spoke them. Their memory was tied to objects, to the light on that particular day, to the branches of a particular season. They might have a thin, light body or be round and heavy as lead, they could even take on a color, an odor.

She was reminded of a poem by Sully-Prudhomme that she had learned as a young girl. Particularly the ending that had remained impressed in her mind:

> *Souvent aussi la main qu'on aime,*
> *effleurant le coeur, le meurtrit;*
> *puis le coeur se fend de lui-même,*
> *la fleur de son amour périt;*
> *toujours intact aux jeux du monde,*
> *il sent croître et pleurer tout bas*
> *sa blessure fine et profonde;*
> *il est brisé, n'y touchez pas.*

The verses were a bit oversweet and didn't have much to do with their story, but she felt there was a kind of assonance, the final echo of what had happened between them; and she forced herself to remember the whole poem, verse after verse. Finally, she wrote it out in longhand, underlining the last lines in red and put it on Arturo's desk.

But Arturo didn't know Sully-Prudhomme and for a few days the page moved around among his textbooks on genetics and zoology; he didn't know what meaning to attribute to those verses. To whom did the *coeur brisé* belong, to her or to him? It belonged to him, she said; but Arturo couldn't understand and Margot made a little paper ball, crumpling those verses between her fingers.

She also tried going out with a young assistant professor of Francophone literature, an athletic young man like the ones she used to like once, his legs and arms covered with a golden down and freckles on his nose. They made love one afternoon in his bedroom and she forced herself to act the part of a good lover. She even drank two glasses of whiskey one after another. But it was like chewing hay and had no effect except to accentuate her feeling of impotence. With increasing anxiety she realized that she still thought about and wanted Arturo, only Arturo. And she would never have him again; she was even tempted to tell him about her failure with the young assistant professor of literature, but something held her back. Something that felt like fear. Fear of his indifference. Or worse, that Arturo would show himself relieved of a burden.

At night, in the dark, the memory of that terrible fight in the room with the yellow chaise kept coming back to her again and again. The screams, the violence. And little by little the idea began to take shape that Eddy *had wanted* to be found with that passport in hand. It wasn't possible that he hadn't heard their voices, their footsteps coming up the stairs. Eddy wanted them to know that he had *discovered everything*. But surely he didn't expect that reaction. Maybe he just wanted to scare them; to show them that he now had a weapon in hand that he could use to blackmail them whenever and however he wished.

Not the wrath, not that blow square in the face, the thud of that fist against his jaw bone, the blood inundating his chin; he watched it dripping down onto his sweater. Frightened, she ran out of the room to get a towel. And for what was to be the last time she moved her fingers across his face, brushing over his swollen lips, wet with blood.

She never went to the Manning Choir and the young assistant professor soon got engaged to a colleague. She bought a ticket to go back to Europe. Arturo would finish his course at Brown University and then decide whether to stay in the United States or move somewhere else. In the meantime he started going to bed with all the young women professors, assistants, secretaries, and anyone else who showed the slightest interest in him. Summer was on its way and their yard was overflowing with weeds. Nobody did anything to get rid of them, and in the kitchen in the morning while she ate breakfast, Margot watched the birds plunge down into them and disappear making the longer stems wiggle, and the squirrels jump here and there through the high grass and then scamper up the white-stained trunks of the birch trees.

When it came time to leave, Arturo went with her down to New York. And sitting in the corner of a little restaurant in the harbor, over a plate of shrimp, she realized that was the last time they would be sitting across from each other. But that didn't add to or take anything from what they said to each other about the voyage and the procedures to take care of once she arrived in Genoa, to the vapid plans for a future still to be invented. And afterward she didn't even want Arturo to wait for her ship to leave and once she was on board she went directly to unpack her bags without leaving her cabin again until the islands in the bay had disappeared from her porthole together with the small leaden waves.

Later on she never thought about marrying again. A family, more children; she didn't want that anymore. And then another marriage would have amounted to a sacrilege. For sins one can appeal to the mercy of Christ but rebellion is a challenge to his pity. An act of pride. The same sin that had deprived Lucifer of forgiveness. If one fails to recognize any superior authority, whom can one ask for absolution? She needed God's mercy and forgiveness. Felt the necessity to receive them for herself and for the dead, guilty or innocent as they may be. She'd already started to feel that way, though still rather confusedly, in Providence, as Arturo was pacing back and forth on the carpet in his silent shoes and the truth about Eddy's death was beginning to take shape in its atrocious and intolerable scenario. And when she went to Nice and then to Saint-

160

Martin-de-Vésubie, Sospel, Mégève, Valdebor, to get to know those places that had been so important in Arturo's life, what had been confused began to define itself as a mandatory itinerary. An unalterable journey whose unfolding, although at the moment still unknown, was part of a preordained plan like the intersecting lines on the palm of one's hand.

Her encounter with a young priest in Saint-Martin-de-Vésubie had also seemed totally fortuitous; she had had no intention of stopping in Upper Savoy. But when the priest asked her to organize a children's choir to sing at Sunday Mass, she welcomed the idea with enthusiasm and together they began to look for liturgical chants to teach to the young cantors of the parish. It was then that words such as Pity and Mercy had appeared, resembling the shards of glass in the bottom of a kaleidoscope that form different designs depending on how they are moved. They came up often and in a variety of circumstances, evading any precise definition. A repetition that, like a beat tapped out on different surfaces, gradually amplified their meaning, never exhausted and continually enriched.

Pity, Mercy, words that kept her light-years apart from Arturo. Words, he once said, that presupposed victims on whom to exercise them. That actually needed them to exist.

It was Isabella who had first helped her to see the light of Revealed Truth. Marmigna's religion was nothing more than a formal Christianity, continually contradicted in daily life. Like her brother and sister, Margot had been baptized, made her First Communion, and received confirmation. All these acts were performed like pieces of a puzzle to be inserted in the right place at the right time. Not unlike the use of the right tableware for fish or the curtsy required when prestigious guests arrived. Until Alberto's death when Isabella included her in that sort of mystical crisis. And those luminous summer mornings that she toddled along beside her sister on their way to church later revealed themselves to be decisive in the choice of a place to live.

The *katholische Kirche*, built only a few years before just outside of Chesa Silvascina, represented the "point of departure," the beginning of a journey that after many turns would come back to where it started from, from that grass, still wet from the night, that she trod together with Isabella as the sun swept obliquely across the shingled roof of the chalet. As soon as they were out of the gate the water falling from the paddles of the old mill drowned out Isabella's voice, her words lost in the rush of the water and their footsteps on the stone stair leading up to the church. Low and long, more like a house than a religious building. From the little open space at the top of the stairs they could see the lake still in darkness and the cows scattered like little flags on the meadows. She followed Isabella up to one of the pews near the altar and for the entire time of the Mass she looked at her kneeling, the veil over her hair and her big white hands holding a missal with gold-edged pages. Isabella prayed, murmuring the Latin of the Confiteor, the Sanctus, the Gloria, her deep blue eyes fixed on the priest with his arms raised in front of the altar. She prayed to God for Alberto, that He should give him the eternal youth and the happiness he had pursued without ever reaching it. And she certainly posed some questions to God. Why and where was salvation. And what was His will in striking down Alberto and not their mother, as would have been the case in the natural order of things. Their mother who continued to command them and make them suffer. To insist on deciding what was good and bad for everyone else.

The people around them gazed at her, so young and beautiful and so attentive. Promptly bowing her head at the Elevation and whispering to the little girl sitting next to her that she should kneel down and cover her eyes. Their gaze followed her when she went up to the altar rail at Communion and extended her tongue to receive the host, her fair throat struggling to swallow as she returned to her

162

place. She, Margot, proudly turned her head and looked all around. Proud of her sister, proud of her devotion. And when the priest left the altar carrying the liturgical implements covered with a cloth and Isabella remained kneeling with her head buried in her hands, she picked up the missal abandoned on the seat. She leafed through the petal-thin pages, where a minute and dense text ran down two columns, in Italian and Latin, both of them incomprehensible in their arcane language. In between the pages there were little holy cards with images of Jesus, tall and thin, handsome as Parsifal. Pierced, bleeding hearts. The Virgin of the Seven Sorrows. But her attention always ended up focusing on the "mementos," the absurd and vaguely ridiculous name for the Mystery of Mysteries that united the gentleman who died on the Grossglockner road and Alberto, entrapped by a spell in that faraway land of straw and mud. The little card with the gentleman wrapped up in the astrakhan-collared overcoat had a gaudy black border for mourning. It was yellowed by time and held up, stiff, against all attempts to bend it. But the one for Alberto was supple and immaculate, edged with a barely visible thin black line. Alberto was turned to one side as if a voice had called to him just as the photographer was closing the shutter, his checkered shirt open at the collar and his mouth half-open, his slightly beaked nose sticking out against the larch trees of Chesa Silvascina. Under that picture, so reminiscent of the sunlight and the wind on a day when Mamigna's voice and the sharper tones of the girls' filled the air, the sound of Gregorio's rake on the gravel in the background, there appeared the stupid, atrocious phrase, printed in italics: *They who die young are dear to Heaven.*

Mornings shimmering with the burning sunlight that comes down off the glaciers and stops against the rocks; lavender gray lava flows in the sky sprinkled with little white clouds. Reflections of Muott'Ota, Grevasalvas, and Plan de Lej in the motionless mirror of the lake. They immerse themselves in the vastness of the meadows, their skin drinking in the air like milk, still cool from the shade. "The brioche, Isabella, the brioche . . ." almost a refrain as it comes from her mouth. That's her reward for having managed to sit quietly during the sermon as the incomprehensible Romansh language croaked in the throat of the old priest like an out-of-tune harpsichord. For having waited patiently for her sister to finish asking for pity and mercy for their brother buried in Lisasa, in the shade of a cacao tree. And as they walk along Isabella is explaining to her the Gospel of the day. She listens to her with one ear, skipping along the banks of the Inn that runs by like a transparent veil over the stones in its bed (it wasn't until farther upstream, swollen by the water from the glacier, that the Inn turned into a pallid torrent, swift and milky). Sometimes some climbers with a rope wound around their backpacks would greet them with a quick "*Grüzi*" as their boots resounded like crystal against the stony surface of the road. Perhaps they were reckless and brave like Alberto used to be, indefatigable like him in the search for new emotions.

But as soon as they turned the corner they could smell the aroma of the still-baking pastries blowing in the wind. *The brioche, Isabella, the brioche.* . . . She runs ahead, her hand impatient on the door handle. Through the glass the sunlight strikes the soft little loaves studded with grains of sugar, the large loaves of rye bread with the hard brown crust. "Isabella, come on, hurry!" Isabella smiles, tilting her head to the side, surely she has already forgotten the Gospel of the day, the Confiteor, the Sanctus, the Gloria. "I'm coming," the metal taste of the fast on her tongue, her blond hair looking dusted by the wind.

That store is still there, Margot said, it still has the old "Müller" sign on it, and they make a walnut bread that's fantastic. If you're really set on going back to Italy, at least take the Majola pass. That way you can go by and get some on the way. . . .

But Lorenza wants to go down through the Ofenpass so she can see some new places. A desire to leave that has been growing day by day: the valley where Margot has chosen to live is certainly one of the most beautiful. One can feel its splendid isolation, the power of the mountains, the silence. But it is too vulnerable to the shade (even Margot leaves there in the darkest months) and one morning she found herself feeling anxious to see the sun and some wide open spaces. An anxiety that grew with each passing hour as if the valley were squeezing her in a vise.

That's how it must have been for Isabella. If not, why was it that she so rarely ventured away from Chesa Silvascina? Why, if not for the vastness of those lakes, the meadows stretching out as far as the eye could see that seemed to gather into their lap all the sunshine in the world. She herself, Isabella, a creature of the sun; not for the blond glint of her hair or the throaty laugh that suddenly broke through the monotony of the day, but for that sort of spirit of nature that stayed with her through the years in the lovely gesture of throwing her scarf around her neck, or moving her fingers over the keys trying to find that melody she'd heard who knows when.

"Take my advice, go down through the Majola." Margot is leaning with her arms on the lowered glass of the car window. "That way you can see Chesa Silvascina again too." Lorenza looks up, already lost in the search for her car keys and the road maps open on the passenger seat: what do you want now, Margot, can't you see that, to use the words of the old phrase, my time is done?

But the eyes whose honey brown has faded into a uniform shade of chestnut are searching around in the car as if they had to find a place for the walnut bread, for the apple pastries from old Müller. "It's not really true that I ripped up all those notes I wrote down when I was still in Providence," she blurts out: suddenly in a hurry to add something else before Lorenza gets under way down the road full of rocks and stones, "Some of them I kept." "What notes?" "The ones I wrote when I was still in the United States. I kept some

165

of them." Margot has drawn back from the car, only her hands left on the glass. "What is it, a secret?" Lorenza tries to make contact with her eyes but Margot's face is too high up, all she can see is her bulging neck, her small, fat chin. "No, no . . . they're just a few notes, maybe I'll send them to you. . . . Maybe I'll ask you not to read them right away." "Well then, when?" "I don't know, but not now," trying to find the right words, "when everything is a little more distant . . . a little more forgotten," and the hand on top of the car now seems to want to push her on her way, "maybe wait until Mamigna won't be able to find out about it anymore."

"Send them to me," Lorenza said, sticking her head out the window, "send them to me right away, I'll do what you want, I'll wait. . . ." They looked at each other and suddenly they both started to smile like two children who have just broken some rule and make an agreement to keep their infraction secret from the adults.

But when she came to the crossing Lorenza took the road toward Zernez and the Ofenpass. She didn't want to go down through the Majola; she didn't want the walnut bread and she didn't want to see Chesa Silvascina again either. It's not true that places, for one of those mysterious reasons that it's useless to try to track down, retain in their bodies (if places have a "body") the voices and the footsteps, the laughter, the screams, and the coughing fits of their inhabitants. It's false; nothing in places, as with recollections, remains unmarred by that woodworm known as memory. Maybe the only things that are saved are those tiny little insects that somehow survive through cataclysms, hidden in the cracks of the earth (a yellow chaise, a wooden bowl, an old dirndl . . .).

5

Afterward at the *katholische Kirche* they saw less and less of Isabella; she stopped going to church in the morning, even to the point of forgetting when it was Sunday. It's Enrico's fault, Signora Arnitz would say, an atheist and a materialist who only believed in numbers and scientific explanations, and who was always ready to make fun of anyone who turned to the arcane for a justification of the mysteries of the universe. It's all his fault, she went on, if Isabella has ended up losing her faith.

But that wasn't true either. Isabella still held on to a sense of life that took into account the *inexplicable*. She had just stopped looking for answers because she felt it was childish; and then her instinct told her that the answers couldn't be given without renouncing the earthly, corporeal meaning of life. Something that was profoundly a part of her, that was hers just as much as her hair, her skin, her voice. And although the missal with the gold-edged pages had stayed in Chesa Silvascina along with the dresses she wore as a girl, she still left some of the *secret doors* ajar. Even though she knew that it was not possible nor advisable to venture out beyond them. A gleam of light and shadow that followed her around silently like an old suitcase for which she no longer knew where to look for the key.

She taught her children their bedtime prayers, but most of the time she forgot to have them recite them, and on Sunday mornings she let Aldina take them to Mass. All she did was make them put their hats on and give them some change for when the altar boy passed through the pews with the bag for the offerings. Sometimes in the afternoon she would take them to Santa Maria del Popolo so they could admire the big paintings by Caravaggio and she would take them up and down the aisles whispering the story of the *Martyrdom of Saint Peter* or the *Conversion of Saint Paul*, careful not to disturb the people who were praying in the pews. The children listened to her, sliding the soles of their shoes over the stone slabs of the tombs in the floor: noses, mouths, eyes all shiny and worn smooth that it was fun to walk on. Princes of the Church and abbesses with their hands crossed over their habits. The powerful of the earth. As though Death and God belonged to them by some ancient privilege. If there was a service in progress Isabella would explain the meaning of the vestments, the solemn gestures of the priest; but she never stayed until the end, as if they had happened upon a performance that was being put on for someone else; and that might suddenly become boring. She didn't like the smell of incense or the sermons, and as soon as the priest turned around to speak to the faithful she would hurry toward the heavy purple-padded door, letting it close behind her with a puff of air. And then in the radiant glow of the piazza, at the sight of the marble lions with the water gushing out of their jaws like a stream of light, her smile would come back. The swallows high in the sky, the shadowy mass of trees cascading luxuriantly down over the Pincio. But also the rain that on certain winter days came beating down against the cobblestones. Then she would stop on the stairs and let the air fill her lungs while the girls slipped free from her hands to run ahead. And if there weren't any cars she would stand there and watch them as they crossed the piazza and climbed up on the marble lions. When they made it to the top they would wave to her and she would wave back, walking slowly down the stairs.

No one can say whether or not, as she told them the story of Saint Paul being thrown from his horse or of Saint Peter denying Christ three times, words like Faith, Hope, and Charity, which had seemed already dead, started beating their butterfly wings again. Whether or not at the moment she let the heavy purple door close behind her, pursued by the voice from the pulpit, she was trying to get out from under their unbearable weight. Or if at times, lying on the bed, her dilated pupils waiting for the first light, her old thoughts would emerge from the darkness like a procession of ants and those words come back to visit her in the voice of the old priest from the *katholische Kirche*.

When she was still "full of health," as Enrico used to say. When her body had still not shown itself in all its vulnerability.

For the *inexplicable* was tied to the first of her desires written in a beautiful hand with elongated *l*s and large round *o*s. A notebook in which she wrote down day after day her last wishes. *Mes désirs* she called them so they would never sound lugubrious but rather as they might have been spoken by her voice on any given morning, her spoon turning in the cup. And the first, of those *désirs*, was a religious funeral. The last, that Arturo be informed, and she wrote out his address in Haifa, in case Enrico might have lost it.

In Haifa, where Arturo had gone to live after he married Marie.

Their story drops out of sight and crops back up again in alternating phases like those underground streams that make their way down under the rocks and are seldom seen in the light of day. They were to see each other two more times, once just after the war ended, in May of '45, when Margot went to see Mamigna in Geneva and Arturo crossed through the San Bernardino pass back into Italy, once again defying the laws of Switzerland.

He went to the apartment in Via Flaminia but nobody was home and he left a note before going to sit in the sun in Piazza del Popolo. That's where Isabella found him. She saw him from a distance and stopped to look at him with her heart in her mouth. And even though neither of them, for different reasons, would have wanted to, the thrill of seeing each other again, the city alive and freshly liberated, turned desire (the one long nurtured in Isabella's thoughts and the one Arturo thought he had forgotten) into two waves crashing together. As soon as they touched and squeezed each other's hand, their lips brushing over their cheeks in what was supposed to be an affectionate greeting, the desire was reborn with the same blind, blunt intensity. Then that was all they wanted, and they wanted it now. Suddenly nothing else mattered.

But the second, and last time it was she, Isabella, who fixed the appointment at the café on the Tiber river drive and the only thing left up to Arturo was the choice to sit inside among the empty tables. It was the winter of '47, not long after he left the United States to reunite with the little boy and Marie, and he had come all the way down to Rome from Marseilles in one of those crowded trains that still took over twenty hours on the journey from France. To see her, touch her, and maybe more. But there was nothing more.

They started talking quietly but after a few minutes the tone turned higher as if something inside them no longer wanted to have a part in that play. Arturo explained what he had decided to do with his life and she nodded, absorbed in drinking from the cup in little sips, the coffee coloring the corners of her mouth. But then they started joking and at a certain point Arturo managed to pull out of her one of her typical throaty laughs, so extraordinary, limpid but sensual, her fingertips rubbing against the marble table top as if she had to judge its quality, seek out its creamy yellow interstices; her short, manicured nails scoring its wooden border.

She had cut them before going out and then buffed them again with a chamois. She had put her makeup on and combed her hair, pulling the brush through several times to make it airy and light. She had chosen the most becoming among the foulards and scarves piled up in her dresser, and changed purses, dumping the contents of the old one out on the bed.

Sometime later Arturo would attempt to reconstruct what they had said to each other in those two hours. At a certain point some ghostly white globe lamps lit up on the walls and she looked tired, the lipstick almost completely faded from her lovely, pointed lips.

Their conversation proceeded with rapid exchanges, died down, and then rekindled again as if what they said had no value in and of itself but was only meant to fill a space. The only thing that really mattered was their bodies, there, at that table. Mine and yours, even if they will never again be one. She rested her chin on her hand, and her arm sticking out from her sleeve sat smooth and round on the marble table top, thinning as it moved up toward her wrist. The same arm was continually traversed by the harsh glint of a bracelet that she constantly moved up and down as she asked how was this Marie, if she was tall, if she had dark hair, if she loved music. She wanted to know about the little boy too; and at a certain point Arturo grabbed her arm to get her to stop playing with that bracelet, force her to look into his eyes and return with her thoughts at least for a moment to that room at the top of the stairs with the water spots on the walls where a sharp, piercing sun poked its way through the battered wooden shutters. To the devil with Hitler: 10 May 1945.

The date was written on one of those sepia postcards that are sold in tobacco shops, with the name of the piazza in italics and the shabby print of a bell tower and a fountain. But she hates memories that are pasted over with nostalgia; that postcard is thrown into a drawer together with the creased photographs of Alberto and Mamigna. Although she would keep the comb in its bordeaux imitation leather case next to her on the bedside table right up to the end.

What kind of present can one give to a woman after two years of being away, when the shop windows are empty and one's pockets as well? The roads are nothing but holes and fording the rivers an adventure, the army jeep about to overturn at any moment into a ditch and unexploded mines poking up through the rocks and dust. Arturo had got a ride by offering to serve as an interpreter for a group of soldiers on a mission to Rome, and Isabella had lied, her fearless intense blue eyes fending off Enrico's questions about that unannounced meeting with her mother's financial manager. "La Semiramide?" he asked astonished, "What does she want from you?" Her fingers described an imaginary letter with stamps and cancellation marks from the Swiss postal service, her *allumeuse* smile languishing on her slightly long chin. As though to say that she too had a right to her relatives and to their news, to know what had become of the small income left to her by the gentleman with the astrakhan collar who had died so long ago in an accident on the Grossglockner road.

An encounter that although it marked the end of an impossible love affair, also united them in one last moment of total pleasure. A belonging to each other that at the same time it was being denied manifested itself in all of its explosive force, that silly little comb in the bordeaux case destined to become a fetish. Never, not even during their first encounters, had loving meant abandoning themselves so completely, body and mind, to desire, a kind of short circuit flowing in their pulsing blood, devouring all thought. An encounter that lasted an entire afternoon and then on into the evening in that room with the battered old shutters and the coarse sheets that no iron had ever touched and that crinkled in the dark, the water marks on the ceiling; and afterward, when the sunset sliding across the wall suddenly turned into the deep blue of night, the intensity of the emptiness that follows such gratification rendered their senses as limpid as if they'd been immersed in water. It was then, amid the voices coming up from the street and the indistinct sound of a gramophone in the distance, that Arturo suddenly found the words to bring him out of the silence that had followed him around like a faithful dog from one place to another.

She had started getting dressed again, sitting on the side of the bed. "Eddy," Arturo said. And after the first trying words the others followed as if they were gliding on rails, one after another, faster and faster, his gaze on the black straps of her slip dividing her

172

smooth back, where he seemed to notice for the first time the light procession of vertebrae. He told of when he had found him rummaging through his room, the passport that Eddy had tried to hide and how he had ripped it out of his hands.

"Eddy?" she asked in a gasp. She turned around, frightened. "I killed him." He had finally told her, now someone knew (but she wasn't *someone*). She gathered herself up as though she were cowering in the bed. She was cold and he embraced her and as he embraced her he realized that he had "catapulted" down through the San Bernardino pass (so Margot would later say) and then tried by any means possible to reach Rome, just for this. His instinct hadn't betrayed him. She was capable of bending down over his words just as the parish priest in Chedde had bent down to medicate and bandage the wounds on his feet. And without looking at her, with his fingers squeezed around hers, their mouths so close together they could feel each other's breath, he told her of when he had caught up to Eddy standing there waiting for the postal coach and how Eddy had tried to run, but he was faster and caught up with him. Eddy had defended himself like a bear, biting and kicking him before falling on his face in the snow. Then he jumped on top of him and kept his head pressed down until he felt the strength of that big body give way. He pressed and pressed with all of his weight and in one final effort the back underneath him arched upward and the head tried so hard to lift itself up off the ground that it almost broke his wrists, the mouth already full of snow hurling out a scream, just one. Then the back remained motionless, bulging in the fur jacket, the legs spread wide, but he kept on pressing with all the weight of his body, his fingers sinking into the hair and then deeper and deeper under the snow. His hands were numb from the cold, they felt like pieces of wood. And his brain felt as if it had stopped working too. He could see in the distance the light of the street lamps shining through gusts of snow and he was totally unable to think. Death had already entered his life from all

173

sides, and horror, but in that moment it was as if the death and horror were also making their way inside him, to squat inide the warmth of his gut. And although it was scary, it also seemed right somehow. Nobody should be spared. Not Eddy, not him. Nobody had any right to be saved anymore. Nobody, maybe not even that little boy who had lived with him and Marie in Rue de la République. Death was in his nostrils, in his mouth, in his stomach, and the nausea was terrible. It was then that he saw the blood. It must have started flowing again from Eddy's mouth when he pushed him down and now it was soaking darkly into the snow under his hands. Then the headlights of the postal coach appeared on the other side of the bridge, and the driver got out to stoke up the charcoal. He waited there motionless until the yellow silhouette of the coach had disappeared around the curve toward Silvaplana, and when the road was deserted again, he pushed the body down the bank into the Inn. Only then, when the body was already in the water, did he remember to look through the pockets, and he found the sheet of paper with his name and passport number just as the current ripped the body out of his hands. The way back to Chesa Silvascina took forever. He felt pain all over his body from the physical effort, his arms and legs shaking. As soon as he got to his room he threw himself on the yellow chaise and started to dream. When he opened his eyes again Margot was bending over him, asking him if he'd been able to catch up with Eddy. No, he answered, there was nobody out there on the road, the postal coach had already gone. . . .

Lying had come easily, Margot believed anything he told her. Then we have to leave here immediately, she said, he's certainly already gone to the Canton Police; and she started emptying out the drawers, overcome with agitation. That night they made it as far as St. Moritz, walking along the side of the lake at the edge of the woods. He started out pulling a sled piled with their baggage but on the way he had to hand over the ropes to Margot; he had no strength left. She pulled and sang in a low voice to keep his courage up. She was beautiful and strong, like a wolf cub in the snow. In St. Moritz they waited in the station for the first train out in the morning to Coira. He fell asleep again on the bench and kept reaching out for her in his sleep to make sure she was still there beside him.

Later on, once they'd arrived in Coira and then in Fribourg, and still later in Lausanne, he never found the courage to tell her the truth. Margot was a young girl who still thought that Joan of Arc had the heart of Snow White; Margot didn't know the difference between William Tell and the Angel Gabriel, she'd never be able to understand. . . .

"You're wrong," Isabella held him tight against her body, her legs reaching out for his, long and tenacious, "but you'll see, Margot will understand too" (and she tried to say that without feeling the pain) "Margot will understand too. . . ." Her eyes that once they were close seemed to light up the object they were looking at, now seemed to enter into his thoughts, touch them and move away and then come back to touch them again. Without asking any questions; not about why we get trapped inside a maze and can't turn back or even stop ourselves from going ahead; not about why one loves and then suddenly doesn't love anymore; how thoughts, desires go in other directions and seem to accelerate, faster and faster. Nor why horror, instead of generating pity, destroys it. Crushes it like an insect; like a flea.

Arturo would later recall with precision some details of their last meeting on the Tiber drive: the imitation marble column behind her head, the cup that Isabella turned in her hands before lifting it to her mouth. The wave of hair on her forehead (hair that was darker, as if it were wet). The little brown appointment book where she wrote down his address, in case she should ever come to Israel. Other details, a lot of them, had been lost, his memory didn't have

175

any more room for them, enough presence of mind to record them. It happens that way sometimes with a painting when the viewer has to choose between inertly absorbing the emotion and actively trying to figure out a way to transform the image into something less fleeting. As if in order to exist in its entirety an emotion needed all the senses and one's whole body and mind. But some of the details had, so to speak, broken off to serve as markers or points of reference. Like the blush that spread over her face when he reminded her of the scarf that had been burned by the heat of the lamp next to the bed.

It wasn't a scarf, she corrected him immediately, but a foulard. It looked like a scarf to me, he insisted, anyway whatever it was, a scarf, a foulard, it doesn't make any difference. . . . It had happened in the room at the top of the stairs, the night that marked the end of their love affair, when she had used that scarf or foulard to cover the light that seemed too violent. But before they left the room, he took it out of the waste basket where it had been thrown away, without really knowing why. Or rather he knew very well why. . . . "A foulard," he repeated harshly, and the blush rose up to her temples as if it were radiating outward from her cheeks, something that penetrated violently into her fair complexion, something that was quite exciting. "Don't worry," he reassured her, "afterward I left it in a bar, before I even got back to Trieste." It hadn't seemed fair to him to keep it, not fair to Margot, but he doesn't say that. Isabella opened her lips to add something but she stopped when she noticed the waiter coming over to their table and Arturo saw her eyelids flutter with that little tick of hers that he knew so well, that blush that she felt was so horrible, that was horrible as the waiter stood there holding the tray with the empty cups. Then the tension eased, Arturo reached his hand into his pants pocket to get out his wallet and pay the bill, and Isabella leaned back against her chair. "God," she said, "if that foulard had caught on fire, it really could have happened . . . " and as she smiled the blush slowly dissipated, leaving the red lines of her mouth, the cigarette that she was crushing out in the ashtray with her lip prints on the tip. And that appointment in the empty café, with the murmuring sounds of the riverside drive drifting inside, went back to being what it was. Just a small transgression. The last.

Afterward Isabella never wanted to talk about that afternoon when they climbed the stairs, their arms still wrapped around each other in the pre-summer light and he had to put his shoulder to the door to force it open; the room came into view enveloped in a half-light with the stiff sheets turned down on the bed. And as soon as Arturo tried to lead their conversation to that encounter in which everything had come together almost as if some kind of magic pencil had connected all the points of the circle, she immediately changed the subject, her face distorted in a frown of boredom. That was when Arturo suddenly began to cry. Isabella didn't say a thing, she just took his hand and brought it up to her face. Arturo spread his fingers to take hold of that face, all of it, in his hand: eyes, nose, mouth, and she pressed her lips against his palm. But about *that* she refused to talk. Not because she wanted to deny it, or for some false sense of modesty, she said. Why then? She shrugged her shoulders, the answer a difficult one, she was tired. "Did Margot ever know about it?" she asked without looking at him. "No, never. Are you glad?"

Yes, she was glad. Her face had turned pallid again in the light of the white globe lamps and her cheeks, which she had rouged with lipstick before going out (her eyes pressed up to the mirror so she wouldn't make a mistake) now looked a little clownish. So many things have happened since that last time in the room at the top of the stairs: that baby, his and Margot's, in the baby carriage in Providence. The little house with the birch trees in the yard and the double-hung windows. The long beach, livid in the dawn light and Margot stopped back there in the sand, she can't go on any further, small and distant, the air blowing in off the ocean cold against her face. Margot didn't understand. Margot couldn't understand. She tried, but her soul was stuck with pins to the Revealed Truth. How could she accept having to change it without making it bleed, without cutting it? Isabella's fingernails run along the interstices of the tabletop, her pupils are two tiny black holes in the clear lakes of her eyes. Arturo entwines his hand in hers as he had done so many times before when the three of them used to go walking down the street, she in the middle between Enrico and Arturo, and each of them had played his part without knowing where that game was to lead them. What was waiting for them beyond the barrier of those days so like one another, almost like the verses of a lullaby.

But in those days her hand had abandoned itself sweaty and limp to his (she kept track of those meetings in her appointment book, marking them with a miniature sun). There was rapture in her fingers back then along with the gratification. Now it is just a big white hand that wriggles free as if she were retreating back inside her den.

Arturo watched her cross the bridge as the car headlights lit up the bottom of her overcoat. Halfway across she turned around to say good-bye again, her hand telling him to write, let her know when he got to Haifa. And before turning around again she smiled at him, without knowing whether that smile would reach him or be lost among the cars and the backfiring motor scooters.

She returned home and helped Aldina spread the tablecloth on the table, filled the water pitcher, lined up the round slices of bread in the bread basket. That *bon-point* that makes such a nice impression on her husband's colleagues when they watch her stand up with a slight outward thrust of her back, which has started rounding out again at her hips. Marta kisses her, burrowing her face into the warmth of her neck, the smell of her skin, like honey and dough; she would like to lick her.

Lorenza has just closed her books. Outside the store lights are gradually turning off and the fatigue seems to condense between her shoulder blades with its smell of ink. She's hungry and when she opens the door to her room her voice sails sharply down the hallway, screeching like a bird, "Hey, don't we ever get to eat in this house!" Her fingers with the bitten nails grab a piece of bread out of the basket and the words read, underlined, repeated and reread, seem to be all ruffled up on top of her head along with her hundred thousand hairs. Boredom, the thing she most detests. . . .

She had finally come to have a cousin (she'd wanted one ever since she was a little girl and everyone talked about their cousins without her ever being able to say "me too"). Really small, that's true, drowning inside that snowsuit in the baby carriage in Providence. But even so it still would have been fun to play with him, treat him like a doll. But then he died before they could even hold him in their arms, what a rotten world! She fell into her father's reclining chair next to the radio, that chair that has taken on his identity, the raised velvet flowers having absorbed his shape, his tobacco, the leanness of his body. "Stop eating all that bread and go call your father. Dinner is ready." Steam is wafting up from the bowls, where little circles of fat are floating in the broth. In the house in front of theirs one of the rooms goes dark as another lights up, crossed by shadowy figures moving against the light. She gets up, puffing with exasperation, her loose kneesocks down around her calves. Her father is in his office putting his notes together. He has to teach a class tomorrow and this year's students seem even more asinine than last year's, he always says, even though they were no slouches as far as asininity goes. "Papà, dinner's on the table," a blue fog has condensed around the burnished copper lamp, the cold flavor of the cigarettes blending with the taste of the bread in her mouth, "Papà, come on, otherwise we're never going to eat . . ." her voice has turned whiny, sweet, she's looking at his pallid profile with the thick eyebrows, the leather buttons on his sweater like little soccer balls: how could she not love him, adore him? Enrico has closed his books, his hands moving slowly across the desk, yellow stains from the nicotine on his fingernails, "Has Mamma come home yet?" "She's home, she's home. . . ."

Once as a young girl, together with Margot, Isabella accompanied Mamigna to the train station in St. Moritz. Back then the Bentley wasn't around yet and they had an Italian car, a blue Astura with white trim driven by a chauffeur with a summer-weight duster. It didn't often happen that Signora Arnitz took her daughters with her when she went to meet one of her friends at the station, but that time there was a small guest involved who was coming to spend the summer vacation at Chesa Silvascina. It was raining and when the train pulled into the station, Signora Arnitz started off immediately down the platform, holding her umbrella up high. The first person to get off was a gentleman dressed in a double-breasted striped suit, immediately followed by a little boy with a pretentious Tyrolean hat and high, dark boots and then, pressing down with all her weight on the footboard, a woman who presumably was the boy's nanny. Last there was lowered a large black oilskin suitcase with leather around the edges. And amidst the other travelers with their bulky sweaters and ski jackets, berets and visors, they immediately stood out; looked a little bit ridiculous. Signora Arnitz rose up on her high heels so as to show off her little round body, still quite attractive, or so she at least certainly believed, and for the occasion she puckered up her lips into a kiss as a long necklace swung back and forth over the rotundity of her breasts. The gentleman took her by the hand and squeezed it tightly before lifting it up to his mouth while she pushed out her bust until her necklace was almost pressed into his double-breasted striped jacket. "Ah. . . . I was forgetting, Isabella!" she then called out as if only in that moment had she remembered her daughters standing under the dripping platform roof.

Isabella and Margot stepped forward and the fine rain fell on Isabella's hair, on her cotton dress and her light sweater. The gentleman looked at her and openly displayed, as if from some irresistible instinct, his admiration. He took one of her hands in his, and in a way completely different from how he had done with Signora Arnitz, affectionately and almost playfully, he kissed her fingers. The little boy might as well not have been there.

Then they got in the car and went over to Hanselmann's for a cup of hot chocolate and the presumed nanny and the chauffeur stayed in the Astura along with the big black oilskin suitcase. Now that he had taken his hat off the gentleman looked almost bald, a few dark wavy hairs that his comb had carefully accompanied behind his ears. He had long, narrow blue eyes, and for no plausible reason, despite the baldness and overlong chin, an extremely handsome face. The face of a medieval knight and at the same time a seducer. The waitress brought over a platter with some slices of cake and the little boy immediately started digging into them, one by one, sticking his finger in the whipped cream and the marmalade and carefully licking it off with his tongue. Nobody said anything to him, only Margot, sitting poised in front of her cup of hot chocolate, manifested all of her contempt. Signora Arnitz was lost in contemplation of the man sitting next to her, and with the excitement of when she found herself involved in some special event, she spoke to him first about one thing and then about another, her hand swinging her necklace back and forth. But her words didn't seem to stir much more interest in her interlocutor than his son's finger, proceeding to demolish one after another the slices of cake; all of his attention was concentrated on Isabella. He seemed flattered to have her at his table and with an instinctive, naïve flirtatiousness Isabella was playing right along, her gaze resting on that neck squeezed into that stiff collar, on those sinewy wrists sticking out of his shirt, and then rising up to meet those eyes fixed on her and quickly looking away. How come? Why all this interest? She nibbled at her cake and made herself look amazed without really being amazed at all.

He, the little boy, momentarily interrupted his excavation of the slices of cake to look through the window at the gray, shadowless lake under the rain. He wanted to know how big it was and what all those carriages were doing and why there weren't any boats and why there was nobody fishing. He had a strange way of wrinkling up his nose, funny and pathetic at the same time. And while Isabella explained to him that the carriages were used by tourists when the weather was nice and the boats were waiting for the wind to come up, he kicked his feet under the table and multiplied his questions. Isabella suddenly felt light, cheerful. She laughed; she couldn't make much out of the lake except a confused mass of color, she said, Mamigna didn't want her to put on her glasses. She wanted her to get used to doing without them because she was afraid she'd end up looking like a governess! She was joking now with the little boy and he was laughing. Margot played along with them too at times, and at times she furrowed her brow, pushing her hard rubber galoshes up against those boots in constant movement under the table. Two ladies at the next table were looking at them: "*Vraiment une belle famille!*" the older one suddenly commented. "*Malheureusement, les deux filles ne sont pas à moi,*" the gentleman responded, politely turning his upper body toward them, "*mais on sait jamais . . . la paternité c'est toujours une question de foi!*" and he offered Isabella a rose, slipping it out from the little crystal vase on the table.

It was at that point that the little boy overturned his cup of hot chocolate. It was inevitable, Signora Arnitz said, he wouldn't sit still for a minute. . . . The hot chocolate spilled all over his shirt, his pants, and he looked up at her afraid. Now, his father said, there was nothing for him to do but go out and get back in the car with

Jeannette and the chauffeur. But the little boy grabbed one of Isabella's hands and begged her with his eyes. He was a chubby little boy, with curly hair, his face smeared with whipped cream, and under the table his legs were now hanging down disconsolate, squeezed into his too-tight pants. The idyll was finished, and the hot chocolate, and so was the *belle famille*.

But it was in front of the mirror in the bathroom. In the bathroom at Hanselmann's, lined with panels of dark wood, where the soap in the porcelain conch shell had that good smell of almonds. It was after Isabella had taken a wet washcloth and cleaned his shirt and pants and then finally his face, when the little boy wanted to hug her, his cheek still wet against hers. Margot forced her way in between them, jealous that Isabella not only got to wash him off but was now holding him in her arms. She pried open a space between the sink and her sister's body, her head with the bow on top now appearing in the lower part of the mirror: above her those two faces reflected side by side, their cheeks one against the other. The round face of the little boy and the slightly more angular one of her sister, having just come out of adolescence. So much alike in their diversity. So much alike in their laughter as the little boy embraced her and tried again to kiss her and Isabella laughed because he was tickling her. Because that sudden passion amused her. The same slightly rounded forehead, the same small, compact teeth and that complexion so quick to blush. The same cut of the eyes (slightly crossed, those of the little boy).

In the European Women Writers series

Artemisia
By Anna Banti
Translated by Shirley D'Ardia Caracciolo

Bitter Healing
German Women Writers, 1700–1830
An Anthology
Edited by Jeannine Blackwell and Susanne Zantop

The Edge of Europe
By Angela Bianchini
Translated by Angela M. Jeannet and David Castronuovo

The Maravillas District
By Rosa Chacel
Translated by d. a. démers

Memoirs of Leticia Valle
By Rosa Chacel
Translated by Carol Maier

There Are No Letters Like Yours: The Correspondence of
Isabelle de Charrière and Constant d'Hermenches
By Isabelle de Charrière
Translated and with an introduction and annotations
by Janet Whatley and Malcolm Whatley

The Book of Promethea
By Hélène Cixous
Translated by Betsy Wing

The Terrible but Unfinished Story of Norodom Sihanouk, King of Cambodia
By Hélène Cixous
Translated by Juliet Flower MacCannell, Judith Pike, and Lollie Groth

The Governor's Daughter
By Paule Constant
Translated by Betsy Wing

185

Hôtel Splendid
By Marie Redonnet
Translated by Jordan Stump

Nevermore
By Marie Redonnet
Translated by Jordan Stump

Rose Mellie Rose
By Marie Redonnet
Translated by Jordan Stump

The Man in the Pulpit
Questions for a Father
By Ruth Rehmann
Translated by Christoph Lohmann and Pamela Lohmann

Abelard's Love
By Luise Rinser
Translated by Jean M. Snook

Why Is There Salt in the Sea?
By Brigitte Schwaiger
Translated by Sieglinde Lug

The Same Sea As Every Summer
By Esther Tusquets
Translated and with an afterword by Margaret E. W. Jones

Never to Return
By Esther Tusquets
Translated and with an afterword by Barbara F. Ichiishi

The Life of High Countess Gritta von Ratsinourhouse
By Bettine von Arnim and Gisela von Arnim Grimm
Translated and with an introduction by Lisa Ohm